Discover
Old Swanage

Charlie Brown on the Quay, 1929. Local fisherman Charlie Brown was also a member of the lifeboat crew, and coxswain from 1934–41. He was succeeded by his son Bobby who was coxswain from 1941–66 and in whose honour the present lifeboat *Robert Charles Brown* is named. During a severe storm on 24 August 1931 Charlie Brown and Bill Brown lost their boats *Neptune* and *Mary Ann*, which were 'broken to pieces by the fury of the waves'.

Discover
Old Swanage

David Haysom

Roving
Press

© 2010 David Haysom

Published by Roving Press Ltd
4 Southover Cottages, Frampton, Dorset, DT2 9NQ, UK
Tel: +44 (0)1300 321531
www.rovingpress.co.uk

First published 2010 by Roving Press Ltd

ISBN: 978-1-906651-04-6

British Library Cataloguing in Publication Data
A catalogue record for this book is available from the British Library

Cover design and walking maps by Roving Press Ltd
The Ordnance Survey map extracts are reproduced from 1926 Ordnance Survey map, 1.2500 scale, Dorset Sheet LVII 9 & 10, Survey date 1926, Edition date 1928.

Set in Minion 10.5/12 pt by Beamreach (www.beamreachuk.co.uk)
Printed and bound in England by Henry Ling, Dorchester

Contents

Preface and Acknowledgements

My first book *Swanage and Purbeck in Old Photographs*, compiled with the late David Bragg, was published in 1991 and sold out within 18 months. So many people have asked me where they could obtain a copy, or was I writing another book; so at last here it is – a new and comprehensive selection of 'Old Swanage' photographs, many of which have never been published before.

Discover Old Swanage is a portrait of the town using old photographs, adverts and maps. It shows different aspects of Swanage through the years to provide a social history of this popular seaside resort. Parts of the town not covered will hopefully appear in a follow-on volume in due course.

The book is also designed as a practical means of exploring the town as the images are arranged in the form of short walks. This allows you to take the book out and about and shows how each area of the town has developed. Sections from the 1926 Ordnance Survey map and special outline walking maps help to guide you. The walking route continues from one chapter to the next, so if you are keen it can be used for one long walk!

Some images are slightly poor quality but essential to show older parts of the town that were rarely photographed and have since been demolished. The majority come from my personal collection. I am also grateful to the following for photographs or providing information:

Martin Ayres, Ann Bailey, Janette Bishop, Pat Bizley, Stewart Borrett, Mike Bower, Bill Bradford, Sheila Bragg, Peter Bunker, Val Burden, John Mowlem Burt, Bob Campbell, Margaret Churchill, Brian Clifford, Denis Colomb, Moreen Curtis, David Dalton, Roy Dashfield, Simon Dicks, Tony and Janet Dicks, Tom Dragon, Michael Elliott, Pam Emms, Philip Feather, Jim Farrer, Gerald Fooks, Jacqui Forster, Eric Gosney, Bryan Green, Arthur Hancock, Bryan Hancock, Edwin Hardy, George Hardy, Ron Hardy, Scott Harrison, Julie Hazlett, Andrew Hawkes, Trev Haysom, Les Hayward, Christine Hercock, Jack Hixson, Jim Hunt, Brian Jackson, Dave Kerley, Roy King, Jenny Lazenbury, Helen Lloyd, Alec Lock, Cyndi Mark, Paul McDonald, Georgina Nicholson, Daphne Ostafew, John Page, Chris Parker, Chris Phillips, Jill Pipe, Purbeck Press, Fred Riley, Mike Rogers, John and Sue Rowntree, Peter Smith, Bill Squibb, the Stickland family, Swanage Fire Service, Swanage Museum, Wendy Sykes, Harry Tomes, John Tomes, Pat Trim, Margaret Warburton, Brenda Whitbread, David White, George Willey, Derek Wisker, Eddie Wright, Wyke Holiday Properties.

Special thanks to John Patrick, David Burt and Chris Kaye, who in addition to providing images from their own collections, kindly checked the proofs. Lew Fletcher also deserves a special mention for following up queries relating to particular photographs. I would also like to thank my wife Sarah for her support and patience during the preparation of this book.

About the Author

Born in 1957, David Haysom has spent his whole life in Swanage. His grandfather and father both worked in the local stone industry, and his father's interest and enthusiasm for local history was taken up by David from an early age.

Since 1988 he has been Curator of the Swanage Museum (formerly the Tithe Barn Museum), which though voluntary is virtually a full-time job. His encyclopaedic knowledge of Swanage serves him well in this role. As Curator he interprets the collections and helps people with their local and family history research enquiries, using the resources at the Museum's separate Local Studies Centre. He also leads guided walks around the town during the summer, gives illustrated talks on 'Old Swanage' and organises exhibitions.

David has co-authored several local books – *Swanage and Purbeck in Old Photographs, Swanage in Old Picture Postcards* and *The Last Days of Steam in Dorset and Bournemouth* – and has contributed to most books published on Swanage and Purbeck since the 1970s.

David is married to Sarah, who is also closely involved in the work of the Museum and was the Honorary Secretary for a number of years. She also writes the regular Museum Newsletter and organises local fundraising events.

1.0 Aerial view, 1926. This photograph was taken just before Brook Garage was built in King's Road (during June/July 1926). In the distance the first houses in Locarno Road had been completed (to plans submitted September 1925). Some parts of old Swanage seen here have now disappeared, including The Narrows in the High Street, Ashlar House and the Round House, all of which appear in this book. The photograph can also be compared with the 1926 OS map opposite. (Photograph courtesy of Purbeck Press.)

Chapter 1
The Quay to Purbeck House

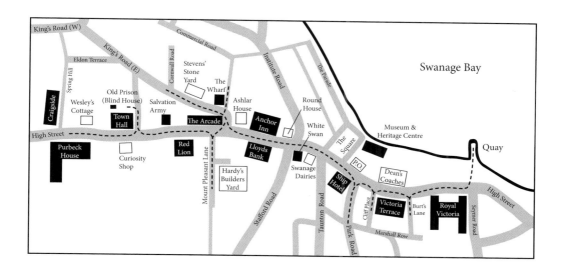

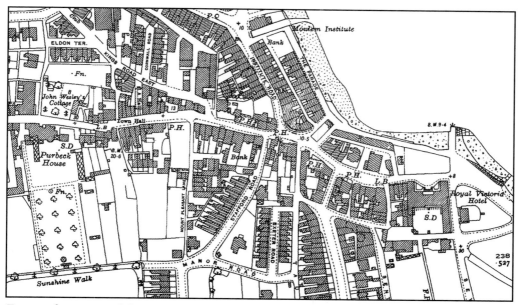

Extract from 1926 OS map.

1.1 The Quay in the 1920s. A Poole-registered vessel is seen alongside the quay. Local fisherman Tom Marsh is on the right of the group by the boat. The paddle steamer at the 'new' pier is probably the *Solent Queen* which entered service in 1889 and was operated by the Southampton Steam Packet Company. In 1940 she took part in the Dunkirk evacuation. She was withdrawn and scrapped following boiler failure in 1948.

1.2 Charlie Brown and Johnnie Brown with their herring catch, 1929. Charlie (left) was also a member of the lifeboat crew and coxswain from 1934–41. He was succeeded by his son 'Bobby', coxswain from 1941–66, in whose honour the present lifeboat *Robert Charles Brown* is named.

1.3 Boats at the Quay in the 1930s. In the background is the Royal Victoria Hotel, formerly known as the 'Great House' and then as the Manor House Hotel. By this time it had become one of 'The Big Five' group run by the Exton family. The other hotels were the Hotel Grosvenor, Sandbanks Hotel, Linden Hall Hydro at Bournemouth and the Hotel Burlington at Boscombe. During their stay at one of the hotels, guests could have meals in any other of the hotels in the group if they wished.

1.4 'Taking it easy' near the Quay. This row of seats was well used before and after the last World War. L to R: 'Siddy' Marsh, James Butler (Headmaster of Herston School until 1945), 'Bidgee' Hixson, Harry Brown, George Summers, Edmund Emerson of 'Emerson's Emporium' and David Lloyd Davies. There are still seats here today in front of Gee Whites Seafood.

. . THE . .

ROYAL VICTORIA HOTEL

SWANAGE.

FACING THE SEA.

THE HOTEL commands a grand Sea View, embracing the
beautiful Bay of Swanage, Bournemouth, Christchurch, Isle
of Wight and the Needles.   Immediately adjoining are
excellent sands of considerable extent, affording at
all times of the tide every facility for bathing.
There are Spacious Dining and Drawing,
Reading, Writing and Billiard Rooms.
Tennis Court. . Produce from
own Farm. .·. The Oldest
Established.

MOTOR   GARAGE.   **INSPECTION   PIT.**

Telephone No. 100.   *Proprietor* **GILBERT V. BUTLER.**

1.5   Advertisement from the 1925 *ABC Guide to Swanage* by Oliver R. Bean.
Gilbert Butler took over the hotel after Miss Isabella Vincent retired in 1924.

1.6 Royal Victoria Hotel at the time of the Coronation of King George VI, May 1937. The central section was the 'Great House' built by local stone merchant John Chapman *c* 1721. The wings were added about 1777. By 1825 William Morton Pitt had converted it into the Manor House Hotel which was renamed the Royal Victoria after Princess Victoria's stay on 7/8 August 1833. The hotel was converted into flats in 1977/78.

1.7 Market traders on Victoria Lawn, 1971. The Royal Victoria Hotel was run by Peter Sutherland from 1965–72. He allowed cut-price traders to use the lawn between 1969 and 1971, which reduced it to a bare site. There had been formal gardens here when Miss Isabella Vincent (and her sisters) ran the hotel. She took it over in 1890 and retired in 1924. A regular visitor Margaret said 'she ruled the hotel with a rod of iron'.

1.8 Steam Packet Office in the High Street, 1922. Alfred Ward (seen here) was appointed joint agent for Cosens and Co. and Bournemouth and South Coast Steam Packets Ltd in 1898. Their office moved here from the old building opposite in 1900. He also became agent for the Southampton Steam Packet Company which took over the Bournemouth Company in 1908. When he needed to contact Cosens' Bournemouth agent or their head office in Weymouth he would often use one of the company's official postcards. The office seen here had been Charles Burt's Stone Office and Weighbridge.

1.9 Jack Ward working in the Steam Packet Office, early 1920s. Jack later took over the business from his father and acted as agent for the paddle steamers from 1946 until the *Embassy* was withdrawn at the end of the 1966 season. Jack also ran the travel agency known as Travelkade.

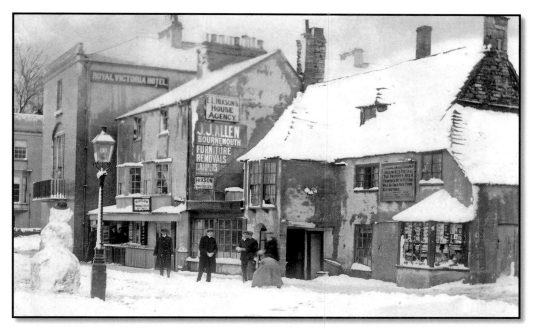

1.10 The High Street after the 'Great Snowstorm' on 25 April 1908. The storm that swept across southern England was the worst any of the old inhabitants could remember. However, by the next day the snow had thawed. The old cottages on the right had been the birthplace of local builder William Masters Hardy who was also a noted local historian and author.

1.11   Seaside Terrace in the High Street, *c* 1912. This view can be compared with the one above and shows the new terrace which replaced the old cottages demolished in 1908. Brown's fish shop had occupied one of the old buildings and their new shop is seen here (second from the right). Beyond is the Royal Victoria Hotel and on the left is the Steam Packet Office.

1.12 Hire car outside Eardley Brooke's House Agency, *c* 1920. Eardley Brooke started his business in 1905 and took over these premises in 1913. The Brooke family ran the estate agency until Harold Brooke's retirement in 1983 when it became Wilcox and Cook. The business moved to 24 Station Road in 1985 (formerly Rose Bros, the jewellers) and then to Tilly Whim Mews off Commercial Road in January 2010.

1.13 Burt's Lane in the 1930s. New houses were built to plans dated 1936 and all the old cottages seen on the left were demolished. The remains of some original walls can be seen

and there is a stone inscribed 'S.U.D.C. 1937' (Swanage Urban District Council) in the garden wall near the top of the lane. The old beach pebbles used to surface the lane were replaced by more regular stone terraces in 1989. The lane is named after the Burt family who had a stone and coal business here at the start of the 19th century, to which they added a bakery and around 1810 established Burt's Stores. On the right is Victoria Terrace (built in the mid 1830s) which has a stone on the side wall inscribed 'Burt's Place 1835'.

1.14   High Street looking west, *c* 1920. Seaside Terrace is on the left with Victoria Terrace and the Purbeck Hotel beyond. The Swanage Motor Company had taken over the Swanage & Coombe Farm Dairies shop as a booking office and their 1917 Darracq 14-seater wagonette is seen outside (probably an ex-First World War army vehicle). On the right is Ward's Steam Packet Office (later rebuilt and used as Swanage Angling Centre).

1.15   Queen's Restaurant & Bazaar, Victoria Terrace, *c* 1906. Thomas Tyrrell (seen here) had taken over the business from Herbert Palmer's widow Mary Ann, whom he married in 1902. 'Lobster Luncheons' were a speciality and in 1913 the restaurant offered 'the best shilling dinner in the town' with 'a pot of fresh-made tea, roll and butter 5d (2p), with jam or cake 6d' (2½p). The restaurant was later run by their children Tom and Julia Tyrrell and closed in 1947. It is now the Jurassic Outdoor shop.

1.16 Swanage & Coombe Farm Dairies, *c* 1905. The shop was run by C.W.T. Dean from 1899–1918. He was nicknamed 'Hundredweight Dean' because of his initials. In 1900 the *Dorset County Chronicle* reported that 'a partridge flew into the shop and was captured. Mr Dean is a licensed game dealer'! In 1919 the shop became the booking office for charabanc services run by the Swanage Motor Company (see 1.14).

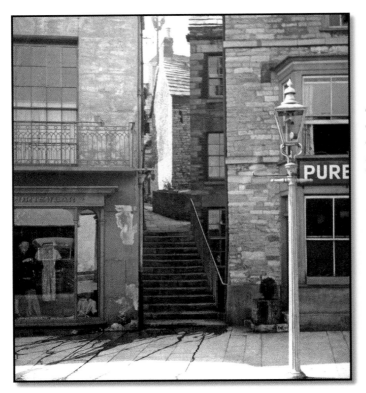

1.17 Cliff Place in the 1930s. The steps to this old lane (seen on the right of the last view) probably date from the 18th century and are Grade II listed. There is one of Panton's (the brewers) boundary markers inscribed 'P.1873' at the top of the steps next to the Purbeck Hotel. The cottages further up are likely to date from the 18th century. Local fishermen Bill and Arthur Dyke lived there in the late 1930s.

1.18 Dean & Son's 'The Swanage Garages', *c* 1933. Their two new Bedford coaches, a 14-seater (left) and 20-seater (centre), are seen with their 29-seater Dennis, new in 1927. The business was run by Reginald Dean (third from the right). The garage was built in 1919 by local firm George Hardy for the Swanage Motor Company, run by Messrs Ruthven & Jackson (later Thomas Bennett). Dean & Barratt took it over in 1924. All three of these coaches were sold to Sheasby's of Corfe Castle in the 1940s.

1.19 Outside 'The Swanage Coaches', *c* 1958. Third from the right is driver Burt Woods, and leaning against the coach is Dean's manager Len Leavis. This coach for the Swanage Toc H outing had been hired-in from Butler's of Milborne St Andrew. In 1966 Dean & Son were taken over by Sheasby's who ran their South Dorset Coaches from here. The garage, later disused, was demolished in 1993 and replaced by Weighbridge Court (built during 1998–99) and Quay House (dated 2002).

1.20 Lower High Street looking east towards Victoria Terrace, *c* 1909. On the far right is the 'Westminster Library' (now Jenkins). Next door is the Purbeck Hotel, built in the early 19th century, and called the 'White Hart' until 1873. The brewers Strong's of Romsey had taken it over (and other pubs in Swanage) from Panton's of Wareham in 1897. The pub's bay windows were later removed, but have now been reinstated.

1.21 Westminster Library on the corner of Park Road, *c* 1900. A wide range of local souvenirs is on display. This bookshop and stationers was run by the Savage family from the mid 1880s until the early 1920s. Alfred Savage's main business was based in Oxford, where he was often seen riding his penny farthing bicycle.

1.22 Park House in Park Road, *c* 1900. This was apparently built as the result of a dispute between two brothers, one of the brothers having erected a similar sized house in Taunton Road, known as 'Taunton House' and dated 1866. On the right is Alpha Cottage of which part of one wall remains. A modern garage now stands on the site.

1.23 Miell & Butler's butchers shop, Park Road, *c* 1914. This small shop stood on the right-hand side of Park Road almost opposite what is now Jenkins. The right-hand end wall still remains. Charles Butler (second from left) previously worked in Southampton and ran the shop (seen here) until he retired and moved to Parkstone in the mid 1930s.

1.24 Lower High Street looking west, *c* 1905. The Ship Hotel (far centre left) was run at this time by the Clark family (see 1.27). On the far right is the new shop for Reynolds the wine and spirit merchants (formerly of Weymouth) built in 1898. To the left of this was the main Post Office from 1901–08, seen in the next photo (now Candleworld).

1.25 The Post Office, lower High Street, *c* 1902. The main Post Office moved here from The Square in 1901 and used this building until a new Post Office was opened in Station Road in 1908 (see 7.59). This photo was probably taken towards the end of the Boer War in May 1902, as there are posters regarding South Africa in the windows.

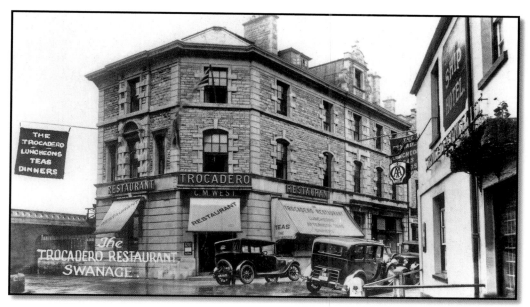

1.26 The Trocadero Restaurant, The Square, *c* 1930. Miss C.M. West opened this restaurant in 1923 having previously had a business of the same name in Weymouth. The restaurant was well patronised by both locals and visitors for whom a cream tea at the 'Troc' was a must. The ground floor is now New Look and the upper floors are flats. It was built originally for the Wilts and Dorset Bank in 1896 but only occupied for one year.

1.27 The Ship Hotel in the 1920s. This hotel has been in business since at least the 18th century when it was run by the Gillingham family. The building dates from various periods and was partially reconstructed after bomb damage in the Second World War (see 1.30). From 1893–1906 it was run by Richard Clark from Leamington Spa. He left the Ship to take over the Bankes Arms Hotel at Studland. During the 1920s the Ship was run by William Hole, and later by Bernard Garrington.

1.28 Taunton Road in the late 1930s. A rare view showing some of the old cottages in Taunton Road being demolished. Behind the lorry is Taunton House (built in 1866) which still survives today. On the left is the Ship Hotel with Hayman's delivery van outside. To the right is the Swanage Dairies.

1.29 Swanage Dairies, The Square, *c* 1930. This building had been the 'Old Bank House'. Charles Curtis added a shop front in 1907 when it became 'Ye Old Knitson Dairie'. This was later run by Dean & Curtis and became the Swanage Dairies in 1926. Many will remember when it was managed by Harry Smith. The building received a direct hit during the air raid on 23rd August 1942.

1.30 After the air raid on 23 August 1942. Swanage Dairies received a direct hit from a high-explosive bomb at 5.16 pm and was completely demolished. Fortunately the Smith family of the dairy was visiting relatives that afternoon and escaped the raid. However, two people were injured at Bick's the tobacconists next door. This building was rebuilt after the war, but the dairy site was not redeveloped for many years.

1.31 The Square in the 1960s. The site of the Swanage Dairies on the right still remained vacant, while the damaged part of the Ship Hotel had been rebuilt in a similar style to its pre-war appearance. The ground floor of the Trocadero Restaurant on the opposite side of the road had been taken over by house furnishers Cundall & Crago (see 1.63).

1.32 The Round House in The Square, *c* 1925. This old property was owned by the Randell family of Ashlar House (see 1.44). It was occupied for many years by James Haysom who was a toy and 'fancy goods' dealer. His wife, and later his daughter, carried on the business into the 1920s. The Round House was demolished in 1928 to allow the road to be widened and was replaced by the present row of shops.

1.33 Institute Road looking north from The Square, 1905. This was known as 'the road to the Institute' until 1884 when George Burt proposed the new name. When the row of shops seen in the centre was completed in 1905 Jimmy Day suggested renaming it 'Commercial Road', but this was rejected. On the left is the old Round House. The lamp post had a sign advising 'Motor Cars' to 'Drive Slowly'. In 1909 a Captain R.H. Scott of Studland was fined £2 for doing the 'excessive speed' of 'over 19 mph'!

1.34 G.J. Chilcott's tailors shop in The Square, 1920s. This building known as Albion Place was built in 1896 and first occupied by tailor Orlando Malpas. It was originally called the Central Clothing Hall and, after various proprietors, was taken over by George Chilcott from about 1914. By the 1930s it was being run by Charles Hardy. The left-hand section later became an extension of Randalls the Chemists, and is now part of Surprise 'N' Store. The Fish Plaice occupies the section on the right.

1.35 Decorations for the Coronation of King George VI, 1937. This view can be compared with the photo opposite showing the old Round House. On the right, Randalls the Chemists advertised that they had been 'established for over 70 years' and were 'High-class Dispensing and Photographic Chemists', with an 'Unrivalled selection of hand-made and hand-painted Poole Pottery'.

1.36 The Square in the 1920s. This view looking east shows the Trocadero Restaurant on the left, with the Ship Hotel, Swanage Dairies and the White Swan Inn on the right. From 1919 the White Swan was run by James Cooksley who was the owner of 'Polly the Parrot' (seen below). His widow Amy Cooksley continued to run the Inn until 1936.

Polly has collected over £350 for Local Charities. When in Swanage, call at " THE WHITE SWAN " and make Polly's aquaintance

1.37 'Polly the Parrot' at the White Swan Inn, *c* 1924. Polly is seen here raising funds for the Children's Hospital in Peveril Road at Durlston. She also raised funds for the Swanage Cottage Hospital. In 1924 the *Swanage Times* reported that Polly's 'subtlety and irresistibility charms the coppers into her collecting box'. Polly was later at the Greyhound Inn in Corfe Castle until she was sadly killed by a dog.

1.38 The Square during the flood, 17 November 1935. On the left is the White Swan Inn and next to it Walter Wright's opticians at Exeter House on the corner of Stafford Road. On the other corner is John Vye's butchers shop (later George Stevens). More recently this was Swanage Music & Video, and is now Curiosity.

1.39 The White Swan Inn, July 1969. The Inn dates from the late 17th or early 18th century, was heightened and extended to the north in the late 18th century, and much altered later. The section on the far left which still survives was threatened with demolition as long ago as 1881 to allow road widening. This view shows the former Exeter House (seen in the last photo) being demolished and the Inn extended.

1.40 The High Street during the flood on 9 March 1914. This flood was the worst for 20 years and affected King's Road, Eldon Terrace and most of the town centre. The estimated loss and damage to goods and property was put at £2,000 and a relief fund was set up to help local residents and shopkeepers. On the left is John Vye's butchers shop and the Anchor Inn with its old stables (far right).

1.41 John Vye's butchers shop in the 1930s. This business began in 1875, and although John Vye died in 1911, the shop remained Vye's until after George Stevens took it over in August 1947 (together with Fred Vye's butchers shop further up the High Street). Members of the Stevens family had shops throughout the south of England including Sherborne, Andover, Newport (on the Isle of Wight) and Reading.

1.42 The Anchor Inn in the 1920s. It had once served as a posting inn and market house. During the late 18th century local men barricaded themselves in to evade the press gang. When Elijah Vacher was the licensee in the mid 19th century he provided 'conveyances for hire' and was also the proprietor of the sole bathing machine.

1.43 The High Street flooded, 17 November 1935. Crowds gather to watch the flood, also notice the rowing boat in the centre. On the right is Lloyds Bank and the Huon Pine Café, and on the far left the entrance to Ashlar House (see next photo). This building stood on the site of the present library.

1.44 Ashlar House, High Street, *c* 1900 (now the site of Swanage Library). In the mid 19th century stone merchant Thomas Randell bought the previous house from Dr

Henry Delamotte. The roof timbers of the house were reused in this new building. As it differed in plan, two separate staircases had to be made to get access from the first floor to the two sets of upper rooms separated by the roof valley. The house, as rebuilt, was called Ashlar House because it was constructed in squared ashlar masonry.

1.45 Ashlar House at the time of the Coronation, May 1937. Thomas Randell and later his widow Emma carried on a stone and coal business during the 19th century. The garden gate at the rear provided access to the coal yard. George Horlock took over the coal business in 1888. The last member of the Randell family occupied the house until 1936. It was demolished in 1938 when Mr H. Cooper submitted plans for four shops, but these were turned down by the Town Council.

1.46 Static water tank on the Ashlar House site, *c* 1945. During the Second World War a static open water tank was built on this site and at other locations in Swanage to help the Fire Service deal with fires caused by air raids. Part of one of these tanks is now incorporated as a garden feature at the top of Cecil Road.

1.47 Ashlar House site after removal of the static water tank, late 1940s. In 1947 Dean & Son submitted an application for a coach station here, but this was not approved. Mr H. Cooper again submitted plans for shops in 1949, but these were also turned down. The site remained as waste ground until the library was built in 1965.

1.48 Swanage Library, 1965. Jefferson Pond of Swanage was the general contractor for the whole project and tendered £22,506 for the work. This innovative design required extra support to the radial roof structure before it could be completed. The central ceramic mural on the inside was made by Christopher Russell who ran a local craft pottery and also founded a pottery and arts centre in Barbados. The new building opened in October 1965 with shelf space for 7,000 books. The Mowlem Institute previously housed the library.

1.49 Silver Fish Grill, The Wharf, *c* 1948. This view was taken after Russell Parsons had converted the building. Where the left-hand doorway is shown, there was originally an entrance arch to a yard at the rear (see 1.53). Various coal merchants ran a business here, including Tom Carey from 1902–05. The shop seen here has more recently been Widdowson's the butchers, then Woodward's and is now JJ Moore.

1.50 Bomb damage behind The Wharf and towards King's Road East, 1942. This view from the back of Muspratt's studio in Institute Road shows the damage caused during the earlier air raid on 14 May 1941. The Alderney Dairy and the Bournemouth Markets building in King's Road East were extensively damaged. Potatoes from the market were apparently strewn all over the surrounding area. The painted sign on the wall of the Alderney Dairy was recently exposed during redevelopment work.

1.51 Cull's Garage, King's Road East, during flooding, 9 March 1914. Harry Cull's garage was built in 1913. On the right is The Wharf. Coal merchant Alfred Kitcatt's wooden sign can just be seen over the entrance to the yard. This sign is now displayed in the Swanage Museum. Alfred Kitcatt moved his business to the Station Yard in the 1920s (retiring in 1926), and Cull's took over at The Wharf (proprietor Percy Boxall).

1.52 Cull's Garage, King's Road East, *c* 1919. Cull's was presumably an agent for Star Motorcycles, as there is an advert in the garage window. Harry Cull was also a cycle dealer in Institute Road (and Wareham). On the far right at The Wharf is J.T. Dickings saddler's shop.

1.53 Charles Senior, saddler and harness maker, The Wharf, *c* 1920. Charles Senior ran this business during the 1920s. The shop had previously been occupied by saddler John Dickings. He had been badly wounded in the Boer War but rejoined his old regiment at Woolwich at the start of the 'Great War'. After a year he was sent to Swanage where his family joined him and settled. He was later sent to Sevenoaks to train a Brigade of Artillery but was invalided out due to his old injuries. In 1919 he moved from The Wharf to the Isle of Purbeck Garage next to Gilbert Hall in King's Road and became a motor engineer (see 6.20).

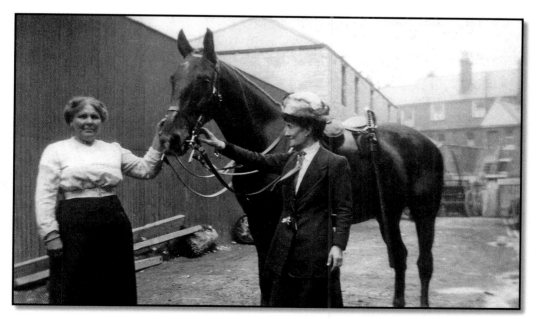

1.54 The Yard at the rear of The Wharf, *c* 1916. In the background is the rear of the shops in Station Road. Cull's garage is on the left. The taller building next to it is now a florists. This area has become the Tilly Mead Courtyard with a number of small shop units and access from both Commercial Lane and Commercial Road.

1.55 Thomas Stevens' stone yard, King's Road East, 1914. This was next to Cull's Garage (see 1.51). The shops in the High Street can be seen in the background. In 1919 Cottees, the Wareham auctioneers, valued the contents of the yard at £1,322 5s 6d. The land was soon redeveloped and included the present row of shops, erected by Parsons & Hayter.

1.56 Thomas Stevens' stone yard, King's Road East (formerly Brewery Road), *c* 1900. An earlier view of the yard just before Cornwall Road was built. The rear of Smith's shop (see 1.85 and 1.86) is on the far right. An old wheel from one of the 'high-wheeled' carts used to load stone in the bay can also be seen in the yard (to the right). The last known example of one of these wheels is preserved in the grounds of the Purbeck House Hotel.

1.57 Cornwall Road after the air raid of 20 April 1942. Three high-explosive bombs were dropped during the raid. One fell here in Cornwall Road, one fell on the Downs and the other at the top end of Station Road (south side) where it destroyed Monty Purchase's shop. There were three fatal casualties which included Cyril and Lily Smith (of the radio shop).

1.58 Cornwall Road seen from Commercial Road, 1945. After clearance of the houses destroyed in the air raid it was possible to walk through to Commercial Road from Cornwall Road. The houses were later rebuilt and new workshops built in Commercial Road. These workshops have since been converted for use by a wide variety of different businesses. The stone building on the right is now the Swanage Christian Centre.

1.59 Smith's shop, King's Road East, during the flood on 9 March 1914. The *Swanage & Wareham Guardian* reported that the shop front was broken by the 'force of the water' which flooded 'the shop and the basement store to a depth of 3 ft, doing very considerable damage to the stock to the value of about £200'. The window was also broken in the 1935 flood and Miss Barbara Smith was injured by falling glass while endeavouring to salvage some of the goods in the shop.

1.60 Stevens' yard, King's Road East, during the same flood, 1914. The *Swanage & Wareham Guardian* stated that 'many of the people had no time to get food or fuel upstairs, and during the afternoon boats were plying to and fro along the roads carrying coal, bread, milk and other necessaries. Workmen were taken home by boat and had to climb in through their bedroom windows. Many a cottager's home has been partially ruined'. The shops in the next photo were built on the site of the stone yard seen here.

1.61 King's Road East during flooding, 17 November 1935. The *Swanage Times* reported that rowing boats were manned by 'local fishermen and police' who conveyed food and fuel to families 'imprisoned in their bedrooms'. On the right are the Alderney Dairy and Bournemouth Markets, both later damaged in the air raid on 14 May 1941 (see 1.50). The Bournemouth Markets was completely rebuilt after the war (later the King's Bar).

1.62 King's Road East and High Street during flooding in 1935. The *Swanage Times* called this 'The Great Flood of Swanage' and the 'worst flooding in the history of the town'. Among the crowd are (by the boat) Alf Chinchen (lifeboat mechanic), Wilson Chinchen (worked at Cassell's), Harry Chinchen (fire brigade), the boy to the right is Denis Colomb, and the tall man wearing a macintosh and so'wester (second from right) is Stan Fordham (watchmaker).

1.63 Cooper Bros, grocers and provision merchants, High Street, *c* 1910. George and John Cooper established Cooper Bros in 1902, moving to these newly built premises in 1904. They also had a shop at Corfe Castle and were noted for 'mild cured bacon and Dorset butter'. Their Swanage shop became Abbott's Stores in 1913. In more recent years this shop has been Cundall's, soft furnishers and drapers, the Antiquarian Bookshop, a fireplace shop and now Ellis Jones solicitors.

1.64 Rose Bros jewellers, High Street, early 1920s. Alvan Rose is seen here shortly before he moved to new premises in Station Road built in 1924 next to the Central Garage, which his family also owned. His father, Lambert Rose, was a watch repairer and had started his business in Swanage in a cottage next to the Town Hall, before moving in 1896 to newly built premises across the road at No. 2 York Buildings. Lambert Rose also traded at various times as an optician, clothier and cycle dealer – a curious mixture! The jewellery shop in Station Road was carried on by Lambert's grand-daughter Daphne and her husband Morris Ostafew until October 1985.

1.65 High Street looking east in the early 1920s. On the left is 'The Arcade' (now Earthlights), built in 1895/96 for Dorchester-based photographer Walter Pouncy. Behind the trees was Ashlar House, and beyond this is the Anchor Inn. The shops on the right were built by Stevens & Hardy in 1902/03. On the corner of Mount Pleasant Lane was Tatchell's Boot Stores.

1.66 Tatchell's Boot Stores, High Street, 1904. This rare interior view was taken just after Tatchell's had moved from a shop in 'The Narrows', further up the High Street. The earlier shop was called 'Tatchell's Boot Warehouse', where they had been in business for over 30 years. Tatchell's moved to Institute Road in 1980 and closed in 1989 when the shop became the Alliance & Leicester and then Ladbrokes (next to the NatWest Bank).

1.67 Mount Pleasant Lane, 1924. This lane runs south from the High Street. Tatchell's Boot Stores was on the bottom right-hand corner. The old blacksmith's shop in the High Street is also visible. The gentleman on the motorcycle is George Hardy who ran the local building firm here, which retained his name until closure in 1985.

1.68 Mount Pleasant Lane, *c* 1905. Previously known as Bull House Lane. Caroline Hardy recalled in 1945 that Walter White renamed it 'having purchased the land and built a house which he named "Mount Pleasant" at the top of this lane'. Hardy's builders yard was behind the buildings on the right.

1.69 Hardy's Central Works, Mount Pleasant, 1985. William Masters Hardy started the building firm in 1864. The yard moved here from Spring Hill in 1900. 'W.M.' as he was known was also a local historian and author. His son George Hardy took over the firm followed by his son Tom and grandsons Llew and Ron Hardy. The business closed in March 1985 and the site was redeveloped as flats named appropriately Hardy Court.

1.70 Hardy's Central Works, Mount Pleasant, 6 July 1985. This view was taken during Cottees auction sale of the contents of the yard and buyers can be seen taking away lots. A display featuring W.M. Hardy's own patent 'Slate Punching Machine', together with the firm's handcart and many old tools and signs, can be seen in the Swanage Museum. These artefacts were kindly donated by Llew and Ron Hardy.

1.71 High Street looking west, *c* 1903. On the left is Walter Pouncy's photographic studio, opened in January 1888 with Thomas Powell as manager. Next door had been George Beer's shop until 1902 (see 7.72). Beyond this were cycle agents Nichols & Son from 1898–1907 (see also 6.12). On the right was Charles Smith's blacksmith's forge and, further along, Arthur Stanley's carpentry and picture framing studio (see 1.77 and 1.78).

1.72 High Street on Coronation Day, 12 May 1937. This can be compared with the earlier photo above. On the left is Tatchell's Boot Stores and next to this is Robsons the grocers who had their new shop built on the corner of Mount Pleasant Lane in 1930. They were a Bournemouth-based firm and traded here until 1972 (their name is still in the shop doorway). On the right can be seen Lloyds the Chemists (see 1.74) and Cassell's fish shop. Note the High Street still had two-way traffic.

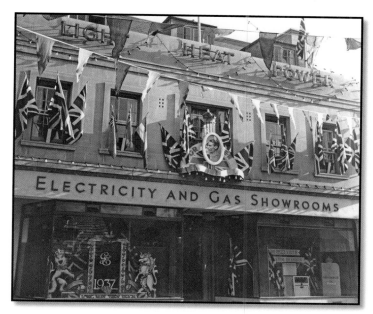

1.73 Electricity and Gas Showrooms, High Street, 1937. The Gas & Electricity Company had just moved from Station Road into these new showrooms. They offered 'Cookers, Fires, Water heaters, etc.', advertising that 'When a Housewife turns to Gas, Labour turns to Leisure'. This shop is currently Purbeck Electrical Ltd (formerly Purbeck Lighting).

1.74 Lloyds Dispensing Chemists, *c* 1950. Kathleen Lloyd (right) and her daughter Mary are seen here outside the shop. The business was started by Henry Lloyd in April 1932, but he died suddenly in December 1933 and the shop was then carried on by his widow, Kathleen. Their daughter Mary ran the shop in later years until she died in 1994. The shop finally closed in December 1995. More recently it became Windjammers Café. There is a re-creation of the chemist's shop in Swanage Museum which includes many of the original shop fittings, together with the labelled chemist's bottles, weighing scales, pill-making machine and other pharmaceutical items.

1.75 **C o r o n a t i o n decorations in the High Street, 1937.** Lloyds Dispensing Chemists is on the left with a flag advertising 'Selo Film'. The Red Lion was originally a farmhouse, probably dating from the 17th or early 18th century. According to W.M. Hardy in *Old Swanage & Purbeck* (1908), the earlier farmhouse stood at 'the west end of the Red Lion yard', with a well, pump and drinking trough close by. In front of the old house 'stood the barn, running east and west, the north wall being situated about three feet further back than Mr Parry's shop front' (see 1.81).

1.76 'Bournemouth Rambler' charabanc 'No. 1' in the High Street, *c* 1922. This was operated by Ransom & Monckton who amalgamated with William Whitelock's 'Shamrock' coaches in April 1924 to form 'Shamrock & Rambler', thereby presenting a greater challenge to Elliott's 'Royal Blue' services. Note the solid tyres of this charabanc, which is seen outside what became Lloyds the Chemists.

1.77 Arthur Stanley's picture framing studio, High Street, *c* 1925. This shed had been built in 1897 as a cycle store for Lambert Rose and was taken over by Arthur Stanley in 1899. Apparently the marks left by handlebars resting on the panelling in the shop could be seen for many years. Surprisingly the shed has survived, having been used by a wide variety of different businesses over the years.

1.78 Arthur George Stanley in his studio, 1948. He was born at Sturminster Newton. After working for photographer Walter Tully in Glastonbury, he became a carpenter and later carried out work at Durnford School in Langton. Arthur liked the area and stayed. He ran this picture framing, photography and carpentry business from 1899–1951.

1.79 Parry's fire in the High Street, 15 June 1914. Sailors from a warship anchored in the bay assisted the fire brigade by removing the stock of china and glass goods from Parry's shop. However, it is said they broke more items than were rescued intact! The *Swanage & Wareham Guardian* reported that the large crowd 'considerably impeded the work of the brigade, despite the efforts of Police Sergeant Thomas and three constables'.

1.80 Fire brigade at the rear of Parry's shop, 15 June 1914. They prevented flames reaching Parry's oil store, although a number of cartridges exploded in the fire. It was reported that the 'naval men brought a hand pump' but 'the fire brigade steamer was sufficient for the purpose, and there was a plentiful supply of water'. The shop was gutted, and damage at the Red Lion next door was estimated at £500.

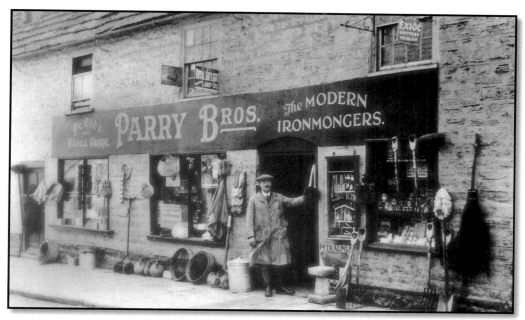

1.81 Parry Bros in the 1920s. The business had been started in 1890 by Samuel Parry who came from Westminster. In his youth he had met Charles Dickens. At first Parry opened a grocer's shop before turning to ironmongery and china goods. The shop was later taken over by his sons Fred and Sidney Parry.

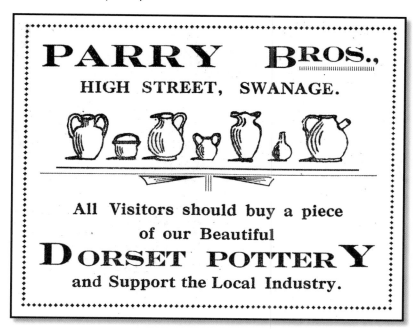

1.82   Advertisement for Parry's 'Dorset Pottery', 1926. This pottery is biscuit colour and non-porous. They have some splendid shapes including both Roman and Egyptian.' It was manufactured at a small works near Ulwell. Parry's opened a second shop further down the High Street (see 1.62) and also sold 'Purbeck Stone Garden Ornaments'.

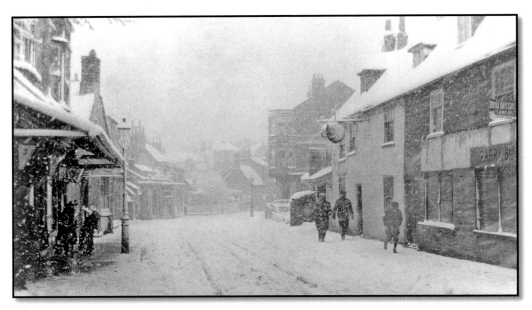

1.83 The High Street during the 'Great Snowstorm' on 25 April 1908. The town had not seen such a heavy fall of snow since the blizzard of January 1881. The weather turned milder and by the next day most of the snow had gone. The old shops on the right, beyond the Red Lion, had recently been demolished, leaving a vacant site for over 20 years until Robsons built their new grocers shop on the corner of Mount Pleasant Lane in 1930.

1.84 Advertisement for James Smith & Son, Grocers and Drapers, *c* 1905. These premises were known as 'Victoria and Albert House'. The Smiths opened their shop at Victoria House (on the right) in 1882 and by 1891 also occupied Albert House next door. The window of their 'Outfitting Department' at the back in King's Road East was broken in the floods of 1914 and 1935 (seen in photo 1.59).

1.85   J. Smith & Son, grocers and provision merchants, *c* **1910.** Staff pose for the camera. George King James (second from the left) later ran his own grocer's shop on Shore Road. Smith's offered 'High-Class Groceries and Provisions' with 'Dorset Butter and Cheese from Noted Dairies'. From 1911–30 Bournemouth-based grocers Robson & Son occupied these premises. Their long glass shop sign with fine lettering and gold leaf is on display in the Swanage Museum.

1.86 Coronation decorations in the High Street, 1937. Swanage was acknowledged as one of the best decorated towns along the south coast. Smith's is on the right, with Cassell's fish shop next door. Smith's is still trading and in more recent years the fish shop became Froud's until closure. It has since been reopened as Swanage Bay Fish by local fisherman Terry Dyke.

1.87   The Salvation Army, High Street, *c* 1937. Originally built in 1872 as a Mission Church by dissatisfied worshippers from the Congregational Church, it also had a Workmen's Hall and Classrooms. Membership declined after 1887, and it was leased and then sold to The Salvation Army in 1936. Today it is shared with the King's Church.

1.88   The Salvation Army Band, 1938. Back row (L to R): Albert Marshallsay, Arthur Barnaby, Ray Norman, Reg Grant, John Stickland, Frank Osborne. Middle row: Fred Chinchen, Alec Stickland, Teddy Speck, Claud King, Reg Chinchen. Front row: Bill Dragon, Fred Dragon, Harry Dorey (Bandmaster), Capt. James Chandler, Teddy Marshallsay.

1.89 High Street looking towards the Town Hall, *c* 1904. The row of shops on the right was built for Sir John Charles Robinson to plans dated 1877. The first shop is William Masters' watchmakers (he later retired to Coventry). Next door is Biggs & Co. wine merchants (of Dorchester) who had a branch of their business in Swanage from 1883–1988. William Millward had the adjoining two shops (see below).

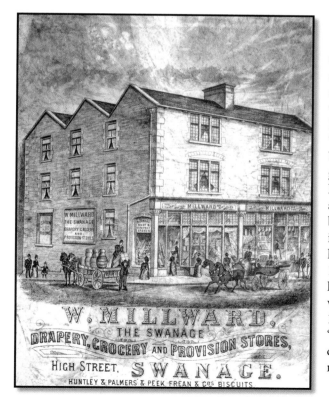

1.90 William Millward's 'Drapery, Grocery and Provision Stores', *c* 1905. This is actually one of the shop's paper bags. William Millward was born at Walsall and came to Langton Matravers in 1877 as the 'first Purbeck missioner appointed by the Wesleyan Methodists'. He gave up this duty upon opening his business in Swanage as a grocer and draper in June 1879. The business passed to his son Edgar in 1907. The shop moved to the lower High Street and closed in 1913. 'Billy' Millward was also a local councillor. When electricity was first supplied to Swanage in 1906, he was in no doubt that this 'would be the light of the future', despite the doubts of other council members.

1.91 The Town Hall, March 1986. The façade designed by Edward Jerman came from the Mercers' Hall in Cheapside. It dates from 1669–71 and was carved by John Young. George Burt had the Town Hall built in 1881-83 and it was originally called King Alfred's Hall. The car park seen here and waste ground (formerly the Toc H Garden) were replaced by the housing development known as Burr Stone Mead.

1.92 Old cottages opposite the Town Hall, 1959. From 1901–14 the section on the left was Thomas Hayward's 'Curiosity Shop', next door was Timothy Hopkins's fish shop, and Francis Hendon also had a grocers here. Older locals will remember Mr Edge's shop, where he restored antique furniture. Following demolition of these cottages, this was proposed as a site for a new cinema in the early 1960s.

1.93 Virginia Cottage Tea Rooms in the early 1960s. 'Open at 7.30 am for early morning tea. Afternoon teas our speciality with Home-made Scones and Cake. Late Evening Coffee and Hot Drinks until 11 pm'. In the garden at the rear was the 'Tinkleford miniature Dorset Village built in Purbeck Stone. Admission: Adults 1/– ; Children 6d'. The cottage was later rebuilt as an extension to the Town Hall.

1.94 The Old Prison, Town Hall Lane, *c* 1908. The inscription above the door reads

'Erected to Prevent Vice and Immortality, By the Friends of Religion & good Order 1803'. The lock-up was 'built by voluntary subscription' following complaints of young men being rowdy. The lock-up originally stood in the churchyard of St Mary's Parish Church, and was also known as the 'Blind House' as it has no windows. It still has its original door, and after the prisoner had been locked up, quarry boys would bombard the door with stones! During the Second World War it was used to store phosphorous bombs.

1.95 Old Purbeck House, *c* 1870. The original building probably dated from the early 17th century and was enlarged by the Edmonds family in 1810. George Burt bought the house in 1857 for £550 and it was here that his uncle John Mowlem died in 1868. The present house was built in 1875 and is seen below. The Burt estate was sold in 1921; however, Purbeck House was withdrawn from sale and remained empty until 1935 when it was acquired by the Sisters of Mercy, a Roman Catholic order of teaching nuns, who started a school here. In October 1994 the house was again sold and converted into the Purbeck House Hotel, which opened in June 1995.

1.96 Purbeck House, *c* 1914. This view shows George Burt's daughter Annie with her dog Silas. Burt's new house and grounds incorporated many relics from old London. The granite globe seen beside Miss Burt was made for George Burt in 1879 and later moved to the home of Burt's grandson Edwin at Beaulieu in Hampshire. This small model is said to have inspired Burt to erect the Great Globe at Durlston.

1.97 George Burt (1816–94). He was the nephew and business partner of John Mowlem. Together they were responsible for many improvements to Swanage, including bringing the railway to the town. The novelist Thomas Hardy met Burt in 1892 and described him as the 'King of Swanage'. Hardy noted that Burt 'had a good profile, but was rougher in speech than I should have expected after his years in London'. George Burt also rescued many old London relics which were brought to Swanage as ballast in the stone boats. There are still over one hundred cast-iron bollards in and around the town, many inscribed with 'City of London' or the names

of the parishes where they originated. Recycling is considered a relatively modern idea, but Burt was already doing it to good effect in the 19th century, earning Swanage the nickname 'Old London by the Sea'.

1.98 Wesley's Cottage, *c* 1910. The cottage stood at 90 degrees to the High Street and was once part of a row of cottages. It was here that John Wesley stayed on his first

visit to Swanage in 1774. He preached in a meadow above Manwell's Lane. Sadly the cottage was bombed during the air raid on 14 May 1941. A carved stone from the end wall, which recorded Wesley's second visit to Swanage in 1787, is preserved next to the Town Hall. This stone was kindly returned to Swanage in the 1990s after it had been found by chance in the garden of a property at Fontmell Magna in north Dorset.

Chapter 2
Craigside to Parker's Stores

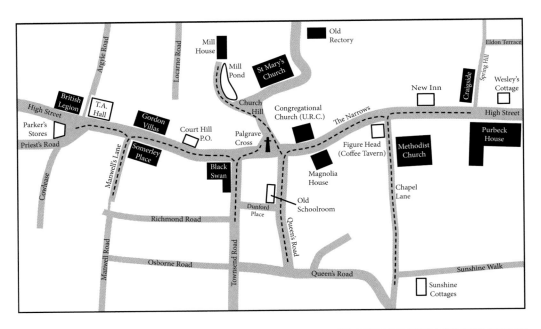

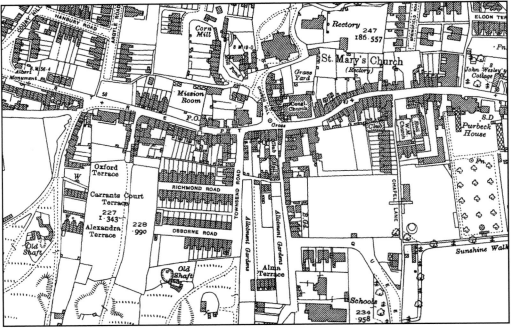

Extract from 1926 OS map.

2.1 Craigside, *c* 1919. This was built by George Burt's son John Mowlem Burt and completed in 1900. His initials and the date can still be seen on the wall adjoining the High Street. It replaced Spring Hill House and the yard of local builder William Masters Hardy. After many years as a hotel, Craigside was taken over by the Holiday Fellowship. More recently, having survived a threat of demolition it was converted to flats.

2.2 High Street looking west, 1937. Charles Hodges' grocers shop and 'Household Store' is on the right. Further up the road is the New Inn decorated for the Coronation. This old established pub was rebuilt in the mid 19th century, renamed The Stonemason in 1971 and was also known latterly as the Stonemason's Arms. It was closed by Whitbread's the brewers in 1975. An application to re-open the pub was turned down in 1976 and it was sold for use as a private house.

2.3   George Green, butcher and grocer, *c* 1906. The proprietor George Green (left) is seen here with his son William (centre) and an assistant. Green's advertised in the Town Guide as a 'Purveyor of New Zealand Mutton and Lamb and best Chilled Beef'. The Green family continued to run the shop until the late 1920s.

2.4   Charles Prangnell, butcher, grocer and provision merchant, *c* 1930. This photo dates from a generation later than the last picture, with the proprietor Charles Prangnell (centre), his wife Ethel and assistant Fred 'Bud' Green (third son of George Green, seen above). The exterior of this building is little changed and is now the Methodist Crosslink Centre.

2.5   Jubilee Square, *c* 1875. This scene is totally unrecognisable today. However, the house on the far right is seen in the previous photo. Jubilee Square was named following the United Sunday School Jubilee in 1831. The row of houses on the left was demolished to make way for the new Methodist Church (shown below).

2.6 Methodist Church, *c* 1905. Designed by Messrs Bucknall & Jennings of Bristol and opened in 1886, it was built largely through the efforts of Rev. George Terry. A large sum was given by George Burt towards the impressive stone spire. Burt's grandmother Mary Burt had walked to Salisbury and brought John Wesley on his first visit to Swanage in 1774. The new church replaced the earlier chapel, seen on the left, built in 1807 (and rebuilt in 1842). This was demolished to make way for the Wesley Centenary Hall in 1907.

2.7 Chapel Lane, 1919. Next to the Methodist Church is Chapel Lane, seen here with Mary Hardy (wife of Fred Hardy, who was secretary of the Swanage Liberal Club). The row of houses further up the lane was built in 1911 (see next photo). These buildings were bombed in two air raids during 1942/43. Builder's labourer Reuben Churchill died from his injuries after the second raid on 3 February 1943. He was believed to have been working on a ladder or scaffolding outside one of the houses repairing damage caused by the earlier raid.

2.8 Chapel Lane, *c* 1934. On the left is Pat Trim (with a visitor) outside the Trim family home. Just out of the photo on the right was the Liberal Hall built in 1913. A bomb fell near the top of Chapel Lane on 17 August 1942 and damaged this row of houses. As a result, ammunition stored in the Liberal Hall was quickly moved. During the air raid on 3 February 1943 a bomb dropped on the Liberal Hall. This caused much more extensive damage and the whole area was soon cleared. The Americans had a field kitchen here when they were stationed in Swanage prior to D-Day. The Youth Centre and Day Centre are now built on part of this site.

2.9   Sunshine Cottages, Chapel Lane, *c* 1934. There were two cottages on the east side of Chapel Lane (also known as Derrick Lane), just beyond the junction with Sunshine Walk. John Newman is seen outside his home at No. 1. The other cottage was occupied by Miss Elizabeth Dennis. The cottages were later demolished.

2.10   Chapel Lane in the late 1940s. The remains of the houses in Chapel Lane and The Narrows were cleared away after the air raids of 1942/43, including the former coffee tavern (seen in the next two photos). The paving stones on the far right are those seen outside the Trim family home (in 2.8). The row of cottages in the High Street (Nos 88–92) had been reroofed, but those to the left were demolished and replaced by new houses.

SWANAGE. HIGH STREET.

2.11 'The Narrows' in the High Street, *c* 1905. The buildings on the left had been built out into the existing road. On the right with its fine portico is Sea View house, home in the late 19th century of retired mariner John Best. According to W.M. Hardy, the house was rebuilt in 1786 and walled in was a small cupboard from the captain's cabin of the *Halsewell*, which was wrecked at Seacombe on 6 January 1786.

2.12 Figure Head Coffee Tavern, *c* 1905. The original tavern opened in 1883 and replaced a carpenter's workshop which was behind the building seen here. The Chapman family ran the tavern from *c* 1888-1900. The 'A.M. Smith' quoted on this postcard view was Alice Maud Smith. Her husband George Henry Smith had previously been a draper and they came to Swanage in 1904. However, following a court case regarding unpaid bills, he was declared bankrupt in 1907. The tavern was renamed the Albany Temperance Hotel. Later uses included the Peerless Cycle Works and Carmel Café. It was severely damaged in the air raid on 3 February 1943.

2.13 The Narrows, 1937. On the right beyond Leavis's shop (corrugated building) was the former Barley Mow pub, which had its licence revoked in 1848. This, together with the two adjoining cottages, survive today. The Albany Temperance Hotel (left) had by now become the Carmel Café, providing 'Luncheons' and 'Suppers'.

2.14 Leavis's shop and Sea View house in the 1930s. Elihu Witton Leavis, 'Greengrocer and Fruiterer', had his shop here from *c* 1918. This corrugated iron building was demolished after the Second World War. On the right is Sea View house. Its portico (seen in 2.11) was removed in the 1930s. The house suffered severe bomb damage and was replaced by the present buildings to plans dated 1949.

2.15 The Narrows looking east, May 1937. Many of these old buildings were due for demolition under the Clearance Orders of 1937, which included the Church Hill and Mill Pond area. This caused public outcry with one owner, Sid Parry, remarking 'it was un-English to condemn the place and give no reason'. A Public Inquiry resolved that some properties would be excluded if they were made 'habitable'.

2.16 The Narrows, c 1950. This photo, taken from approximately the same position, shows the site cleared after the air raid in 1943. An earlier pre-war road-widening scheme had yet to be implemented, making this now the widest part of the High Street. Only the cottages on the left were repaired. One has been recently restored (No. 90 High St.) and shows evidence of having been raised when the height of the road was altered, probably in the mid 19th century.

2.17   The Narrows looking east, *c* 1912. The low building on the right may have dated from the 17th century, before the road level was raised. This was probably done during the 1840s when John Mowlem was waywarden. Louisa Wallington's tobacconists and confectionary shop (seen in the centre) had been 'Tatchell's Boot Warehouse' until 1904, when they moved further down the High Street (see 1.65 and 1.66).

2.18 Magnolia House, *c* 1918. A fine old building dating from the 17th century and called originally 'The New House', this view was taken when it was a 'Board Residence' run by the Misses Garlick (seen here in the centre). Their advert in the annual Town Guide offered 'Moderate Terms' with 'Electric Lighting Throughout' and a 'Garage'. On the right is the Congregational Church (now the United Reformed Church).

2.19 High Street looking west, *c* 1912. On the left is Job Smith's 'Furnishing Stores', built in 1886. They had a second shop built on the corner of Shore Road and Station Road in 1914 (see 7.62). Beyond this was Sparkes' shop which Arthur Sparkes ran from 1904. It was also an off-licence, later became Aplin's and was rebuilt in 1972 (now Arkwrights). In the centre are the Black Swan and Church Hill House.

2.20 Congregational Church, *c* 1906. The original Meeting House was built in 1705 and it was here that John Wesley preached on his second visit to Swanage in 1787. This chapel was rebuilt in 1837, and then, during Rev. Thomas Steer's popular ministry, a new church was built in 1900/01 (now the URC). Rev. Steer retired to Reading in 1908. When he died in 1927, the Swanage Urban District Council named a new road in his honour (see 5.8).

2.21 'Fire Drama at Factory', 1966. This was the headline in the *Swanage Times* on 7 September 1966. They reported that 'Swanage fire service under station officer R.E.J. Paull dealt with the seat of the fire in the boiler room and latex processing department. But it had got a hold on the high roof of Curtis's antique showrooms by 12 noon. Just before 1 pm the fire burst out of the Curtis's building fronting the High Street, sending showers of hot stones and plaster into the street'. This view also shows John Aplin's off-licence (demolished in 1972).

2.22 The Candlewick factory fire, 5 September 1966. This was the largest fire in Swanage for many years and destroyed Ronald Boot's factory and part of Ross and John Curtis's antique shop (opposite the URC). The fire brigade was joined by appliances from Wareham and Hamworthy, but low water pressure at times reduced the flow of water through the hoses to a trickle. Hoses were also run down Church Hill to pump water out of the Mill Pond. The fire raged for over 4 hours and damage was estimated at £100,000.

2.23 Queen's Road looking north, 1915. These cottages in Queen's Road were known as Ashlar Row until 1892. Seen here are Fred Masters and his mother Ann, who was a 'faithful and earnest member' of the Congregational Church. For some years Mrs Masters had been living here with her son Albert who was a local postman. Fred was another of her six sons and had a hairdresser's shop in the High Street on the east end of Handfast Terrace (near the Black Swan). This shop was later run by John Chinchen.

2.24 Queen's Road looking north, in the 1930s. A poor (but rare) view of these old cottages taken further up the road from the previous photo. Note the unusual house on the far right showing the date 'AD 1705'. These buildings were later demolished, but the newer houses on the far left survive today.

2.25 Queen's Road, 1948. This view shows the remains of the old cottages lower down the road from those in the previous photo. Some of the other buildings in this photo survive today, and the roof line of one of the demolished cottages can still be seen on the end wall. The back of Magnolia House is just visible on the far right.

2.26 The Old Schoolroom, Queen's Road, 1969. The schoolroom and other old buildings seen here were demolished and replaced by new housing in the early 1970s. This building is also in the background of photo 2.24. As well as School Lane, this was also known as Hopabout Lane. The ex-London bollard in the distance (by the steps) is now further down on the corner outside Arkwrights.

2.27 High Street and Church Hill, *c* 1929. On the left is the Palgrave memorial cross and Stickland's butchers shop is just past the lamp post. On the far right is the Labour Hall and next to it Sparkes off-licence. Different generations know this shop as Sparkes, Aplin's and now Arkwrights. The old shop seen here was demolished in 1972. Beyond this was Smith's Furnishing Stores, later Curtis's antique shop, partially destroyed by fire in 1966 and rebuilt in 1973 (see 2.21 and 2.22).

2.28 Stickland's butchers shop, *c* 1925. Albert Stickland (left) was born at Totnes and later worked for Swanage butcher John Vye. In 1909 he emigrated to Canada and became a meat packer and lumberjack before joining the Canadian Army in 1914. He returned to Swanage in 1919 and was a 'horse cabbie' before converting Dixon's bakehouse on Church Hill into a butchers. In 1925 he turned Tommy Barlow's paper shop into the butchers seen here, which was carried on by his son Peter until 2008.

2.29 Coronation celebrations, Church Hill, 1937. On King George VI's Coronation Day, 12 May, special events included at 6.30 pm a 'Procession and Carnival' around the town (in heavy rain), headed by the Military Band of the Swanage Music Society. At 8 pm the King's Speech was broadcast, but due to the bad weather the 'Country Dancing' was postponed and the 'Display of Fireworks' was held the next night.

2.30 Old cottage (known as 'The Arc'), Church Hill, May 1937. Mrs Anne Amelia Norman (née Turner) is seen at her cottage in Church Hill. As part of the week-long celebrations, an 'Old Peoples' Tea and Entertainment' was held at the Church Hall in King's Road on Thursday 13 May at 5.30 pm.

2.31   Maypole dancing in Church Hill, Coronation Day, 1937. The maypole had been given by Mrs McCausland and music was provided by 'Messrs F. Parker (accordion), W. Elliott (banjo) and B. Marsh (tambourine)'. Children at the local schools were presented with a book *George VI, King and Emperor*. There was a 'Procession of School Children' from 'Herston to Sandpit Field' at 3.15 pm, followed by a 'Children's Tea' on the field at 4 pm.

2.32   Coronation celebrations, Church Hill, 1937. Back row (L to R) includes: Jean Elliott, Ciss Carter, Mary Stickland, Margaret Hancock, Ethel Stockley, Mrs McCausland, Joyce Hardley, Millie Fowler, Mrs Foot and Annie Marsh. Among the front rows (L to R) are: Margaret Sparkes, Grace Mullings, Mavis Marsh, Nancy Smith, June Carter, Janet Gillingham, Doreen Turner, Joan Bryant, Rosa Foot and Margaret Marsh.

2.33 Church Hill on V.J. Day, 15 August, 1945. Only 8 years separate the photos on this page from those opposite. However, during that time Britain had been through the Second World War. To mark the Japanese surrender, the flag at St Mary's Parish Church was flown at half mast and the Last Post sounded by Arthur Goodey (verger and parish clerk) in remembrance of those who gave their lives in the war. Damage to the church roof during the air raid on 3 February 1943 can be seen, when 14 windows were also blown out.

2.34 Bomb damage in Church Hill after the air raid on 3 February 1943. A high-explosive bomb fell through the organ at the back of the Congregational Church and exploded in the old churchyard. It also caused blast damage to the Parish Church and Tithe Barn. The remains of the old cottages seen here were subsequently demolished and replaced by a single house which would later become the new Rectory.

2.35 The Mill Pond, *c* 1910. The wall of the Mill House at the far end of the pond has a stone inscribed 'BEN BARLOW Mill Wright of Southampton *fecit* 1754'. This probably indicates a rebuilding date as the house shows indications of medieval work. The only early cottage remaining is immediately to the left of the Mill House and may date from the 17th century.

2.36 The Mill Wheel, 1902. A rare view when the corn mill was still in use. John Rawles was the last miller from 1884 until the 1920s. The mill and pond (part of the Burt Estate) were sold to Joseph Parsons in 1921 for £700. Most of the machinery went for scrap during the Second World War. The wheel seen here was removed, but more recently a 19th century replacement (made by Winter & Hossey of Dorchester) was brought from Sturminster Newton.

2.37 The Mill Pond, *c* 1910. The pond is fed by spring water which can often be seen bubbling up by the steps seen here. The high wall was added in the 1880s to stop drunks from the Black Swan pub coming down the hill and falling into the pond! Only the unusual chimney of the cottage on the far left remains, as this and all the adjoining cottages were sympathetically rebuilt in the 1950s and 1960s.

2.38 The Mill Pond in the 1920s. This area was also affected by the Clearance Orders of 1937 when many old cottages were threatened with demolition. This caused outcry and led to an article in the *Sunday Times* which described the plans as 'defacing the beauty of our old buildings. Those that replace them are rarely as good'. Following a Public Inquiry, most properties were excluded from the Orders, but Witney Cottages and Witney House (seen far left) were among those demolished.

2.39 Church Hill and High Street looking west, 1896. The cottage on the far right was later demolished and Church Hill House extended (to plans dated 1901). The board visible on the cottage in the centre advertised Annie Squires' seed business. The parish pump seen here was removed in 1907. On the far left is George Beer's delivery van outside Joseph Brown's shop. Mr Brown also hired out pony traps.

2.40 Church Hill and High Street, *c* 1912. This can be compared with the previous photo and shows Church Hill House after rebuilding work. The cross was erected in 1909 as a memorial to Sir Reginald Palgrave and his wife Grace. Palgrave had been a clerk to the House of Commons for nearly 40 years. However, their family did not want to make the memorial too public, so the inscription on the base was carved in Latin.

2.41 Old cottages on the corner of Townsend Road, May 1937. Some of these buildings were included in the Clearance Orders in 1937. Ruins of those nearest the camera still remained until the mid 1960s when the present houses were built further back to allow road widening. This was completed in the early 1970s after demolition of the last of these buildings, including John Aplin's shop on the corner of Queen's Road.

2.42 High Street looking east in the 1920s. This unidentified local event shows how narrow the road was at this point before widening took place. The houses seen here on the corner of Townsend Road (far right) have now been demolished, although Church Hill House on the other side of the road looks little changed today.

2.43 Town's End Lane, *c* 1901. A view difficult to recognise today, although Church Hill House in the High Street is just visible in the distance (seen during rebuilding). The buildings at the bottom were later demolished and the lane widened and renamed Townsend Road. This is how a number of lanes in Swanage would have looked in the 19th century. Many were used by wagons coming down from the stone quarries.

2.44 Old houses in Townsend Road, 1940s. These houses are on the right of the previous photo (behind the lamp post). They had no windows at the rear, perhaps to avoid the dust and dirt created by the wagons passing all day long through the streets to the stone yards or 'bankers' on the seashore. According to W.M. Hardy they took on average '60 loads a day' and made ruts in the roads 'nine to twelve inches deep'.

2.45 The Black Swan Inn, High Street, *c* 1920. This was originally a farmhouse, dating back perhaps five or six hundred years, although with later alterations and additions. Local historian W.M. Hardy noted in 1908 that the 'farmyard, barn, stables, and out-buildings were situated at the back, and the greater part of them have been recently cleared away'. From the 1790s to 1815 the pub was run by Stephen and Sarah Bore. Members of the Benfield and Dowland families ran the pub from 1838–99. In the 1930s the licensee was 'Bobby' Brown, later coxswain of the Swanage lifeboat from 1941–66.

2.46 The Black Swan Inn at the time of the Coronation, 1937. The building left of the pub was demolished in 1960, although part of the front wall (including a blocked-up window) can still be seen today. Both the raised position of the pub and Vera Cottage opposite show how much the road level has been lowered, possibly during road improvements when John Mowlem was waywarden in the 1840s.

2.47   Vera Cottage, opposite the Black Swan, February 1937. A new house was built on this site to plans dated 1959, although the original steps and the raised section either side can be seen today and still show where the railings were cut off. Many railings in Swanage went for scrap during the last war. To the right of the photo is Vic Foote.

2.48 High Street looking west, *c* 1905. Court Hill extended from here to what we now regard as Court Hill, or more correctly Court Road. On the right is Court Hill Post Office opened in 1901. It was run in later years by Minnie Summers and closed in September 1971 when she retired. Handfast Terrace on the left was built by Frank Burt in 1893 to replace Handfast House (after a fire).

2.49 High Street looking west, *c* 1875. An early view before Gordon Villas was built by Frank Burt on the land to the far right. The tall building on the left is Somerley House (on the corner of Manwell's Lane, also known as Summers' Lane). It was the home of Charles Summers who was a carriage proprietor and drove an omnibus to Wareham to meet the trains. In the distance is the old smithy, later Parker's Stores.

2.50 Day's shop, Somerley Place, *c* 1925. In 1921 Arthur Thomas Day took this shop over from John Rawles, who had been a corn dealer and was the last miller at the mill in Church Hill. By 1928 the shop had been taken over by fruiterer Reginald Legg. These premises have seen many changes of use and it is now Sandie's barbershop.

2.51 Manwell's Lane, 1937. This old lane was named after the Manwell family who dwelt here from the 18th century, including Thomas Manwell who was known as the 'Swanage Philosopher'. According to local historian and author William Masters Hardy, another resident of the lane was 'an old pensioner named Stickland, who had fought under Nelson at Trafalgar'.

2.52 Manwell's Lane, 1930s. As W.M. Hardy noted in his book *Old Swanage & Purbeck*, 'the narrowness of this lane is explained by the many encroachments made, a process of

slow growth'. In the doorway of the cottage on the east side is Frank Haysom, next to him is Alfred Taylor who resided at No. 3, and George Parker who lived at No. 1. At the top of the lane is Florence Stockley's house, shown in the next photo. Note the gate on the right; this led into a meadow known as 'Rusbies' where John Wesley preached to a large congregation on 12 October 1774 during his first visit to Swanage.

2.53 No. 5, Manwell's Lane in the late 1920s. Florence Stockley with her two children William and Florence are seen outside their home at No. 5. Sadly her husband Abraham Foyle Stockley had died in Swanage in 1920 as a result of injuries he received on active service during the First World War. Another family called Stockley had lived at No. 4 until about 1916, before moving to Trowbridge in Wiltshire.

2.54 Manwell's Lane, *c* 1930. This view from the top of the lane shows Florence Stockley's house on the far right. Further down are the cottages seen in photo 2.52. By the 1960s these were in ruins and cleared away to create a car park, but remains of the back walls of some of the buildings can still be seen today.

2.55 Parker's Stores in the High Street, 1930s. This building probably dates from the 17th century. The lean-to on the right was a later addition. At the time of a Chancery Sale in 1823 it was a blacksmith's shop. Harry Linington had a grocery business here in the First World War (see also 5.21). In the 1920s it was a fish and chip shop run by John Jackman until he moved to a new shop (now Wok Chef) next to Manwell's Lane. The Parker's name is still retained (painted on the front wall), but the shop was converted for residential use between 2005 and 2009.

2.56 Parker's Stores in the 1930s. Annie Parker, who took over the shop in 1927, is seen here with her son Jack, who prepared the window display. This was entered into a *Daily Express* competition. Jack's brothers Bert and Ron also worked in the shop. Ron was killed in action in Normandy on 11 June 1944.

Chapter 3
Cowlease and Priest's Road

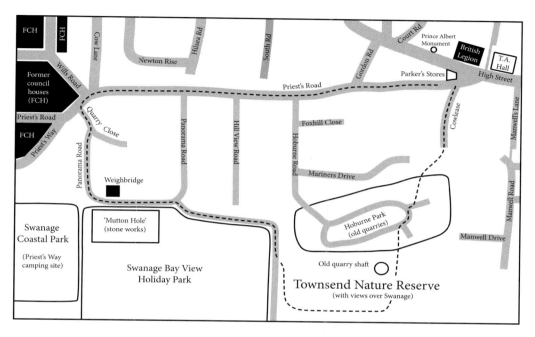

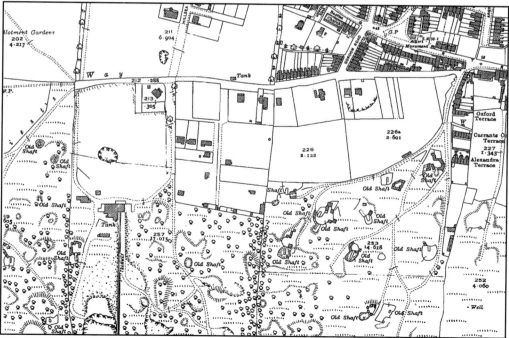

Extract from 1926 OS map.

3.1 Priest's Road in the 1920s. The condition of the road was a long-standing problem. In 1939 George Summers recalled that in the late 19th century, when Joseph Parsons was surveyor, they used to pull down gravel and tip refuse from other roads there. On several occasions repairs had been made and stone rolled in. The top of the road was taken off and spread over the rest of the surface, making it into a fairly good condition.

3.2 Cowlease looking south to the quarries, *c* 1930. According to W.M. Hardy, one of the cottages at Cowlease had once been 'occupied by a noted smuggler, who had cellars in his garden for stowing contraband'. Further up are Oxford Terrace, Carrant's Court and Alexandra Terrace. The top two terraces were built to plans dated 1876 and 1881. On the bottom left, Strong's former bakehouse (dated 1936) had yet to be built.

3.3 Stone quarries at Cowlease in the 1920s. Only a few quarries at Cowlease and Townsend were still in use. Harry Chinchen and Walter Brown were still working their quarry and also George Burt (not the George Burt of Purbeck House). The remains of the quarries were cleared away to build Hoburne Park in the mid 1970s. Some of the better preserved shafts were fenced off.

3.4 Stone quarry above Cowlease, 1914. This quarry was on what is known locally as 'Grandfather's Knap'. It can still be seen today within the Townsend Nature Reserve. The walls around the quarry shaft have been rebuilt, although the capstan rotted away after the quarry closed and the two 'crabstones' which supported it are now broken. Note the poles at the top of the 'slide' to prevent cattle falling down the shaft.

3.5 The Burt family quarry at Cowlease, *c* 1925. In the centre is George Burt sitting on one of the 'crabstones' that supported the wooden capstan. The chain from the capstan is seen at the bottom right and indicates the position of the shaft, which was just beyond the right-hand side of this photo. Local guide books encouraged visitors to make the quarries one of the places not to be missed during their stay.

3.6 Burt's quarry at work, *c* 1925. George Burt is on the left. His horse is harnessed to the long wooden pole or 'spack' which turned the capstan and brought the stone up the 'slide' from the underground quarry on a small 'quarr cart' (see next photos). The open-fronted 'quarr houses' in the background were used to work the stone on benches, also made of stone, and known as 'bankers'.

3.7 Underground quarrying, *c* 1925. George Burt is using an 'endless chain' to move a block of stone. This was unusual in the quarries at Swanage where the ceiling heights were generally only a few feet and restricted the use of this type of lifting equipment. The actual width of the tunnels known as 'lanes' and ceiling height varied throughout each underground working, and is well illustrated below.

3.8 Getting ready to bring the stone up, *c* 1925. The block of stone has been lowered onto the 'quarr cart' and is being pulled along the 'lane' with George Burt helping its progress using a bar known locally as a 'paddle'. At the bottom of the shaft the cart would be drawn up the 'slide' to the surface by the horse turning the capstan.

3.9 Newton Stone Quarries works, known locally as 'Mutton Hole', *c* 1930. This is now the site of Swanage Bay View Holiday Park. However, the weighbridge, made by Samuel Denison & Son of Leeds, and the office (seen here) are still there today. On Friday 25 October 1940 a time-delay bomb fell nearby and part of Steer Road had to be evacuated. The bomb exploded on the following Monday, some 71 hours later.

3.10 'Mutton Hole' in the 1930s. The stone would be taken down to the cracker at the works and then used for road building and other purposes. Leaning on the lorry is Fred 'Bud' Green. The works started in the early 1920s and was run by Ernie Burt. In 1931 it was taken over by Swanage Quarries Ltd and managed by Fred Lovell. The works closed in the early 1950s, and can be seen in the next photograph.

3.11 Priest's Way camping site, *c* 1956. On the far right is the 'Mutton Hole' works (see 3.9), and in the background the newly built council houses in Priest's Road. Beyond this, on the left, is the earlier council housing in Steer Road dating from the 1920s. The long building in the centre is Wilson's removals warehouse, later converted into flats.

3.12 New council housing, Priest's Road, 1955. These houses were designed by A.E.O. Geens and built of Purbeck stone by Messrs Wilson of Bournemouth and Jefferson Pond of Swanage. They were awarded a Gold Medal by the Ministry of Housing for the 'best County Borough or Urban District Housing Scheme in the Southern Region' and out of 'sixty three houses, sixty had gas cookers'.

3.13 Priest's Road, 1954. A view that is now almost unrecognisable. It was taken looking west from a point just beyond the junction with Panorama Road. The bushes and trees have gone, but the houses on the right, built during the late 1930s, are still there today.

3.14 Priest's Road, 1955. This photograph can be compared with the above view. The junction with Panorama Road can be seen on the far left. The house on the corner, built by Arthur Bird to plans dated 1921, was named Panorama and later gave its name to the road. This used to provide access to the Newton Stone Quarries works (later Swanage Quarries Ltd), known as 'Mutton Hole' (see 3.9) and is now the site of Swanage Bay View Holiday Park.

3.15 The Home Guard fundraising in Priest's Road, 1944. They are seen at the junction with Hill View Road (on the right). Back row (L to R): Bert Collier, Bill Redout, Chris Bradford, Tom Wright, Bob Spearman, Bill Fowler. Front row: Malcolm Pond, George Aplin, Bill Laird, Fred 'Bud' Green, Jack Satherley, Bob Cann.

3.16 Priest's Road in the 1920s. This is looking west from the junction with Gordon Road. The long wall is still there and the houses beyond. On the left had been an opencast stone quarry and set back from the road a house called Windspit, built to plans dated 1921. This has now been replaced by Foxhill Close.

3.17 Gordon Road, *c* 1908. This is one of the steepest roads in Swanage. The houses on the right were built by local builder Fred Pond in 1899/1900. The *Swanage & Wareham Guardian* noted how quickly the houses were being constructed 'where only a few weeks before had been meadow land'. Beyond the trees on the left is Princess Road which had yet to be connected with the High Street (see 6.2).

3.18 Priest's Road in the 1920s. Another view showing the poor condition of the road. In 1939 George Summers recalled that the first time he saw Priest's Road repaired was about 50 years earlier and that the Local Board (later the Urban District Council) repaired the footpath in about 1884. He stated that when Joseph Parsons was surveyor to the Local Board in the late 19th century the road was in a better condition than the High Street. Frank Selby also said he had known the road for 50 years, and that the only change that had taken place was when the local council had filled a large hole and repaired the road.

Chapter 4
British Legion Club to
Newton Manor

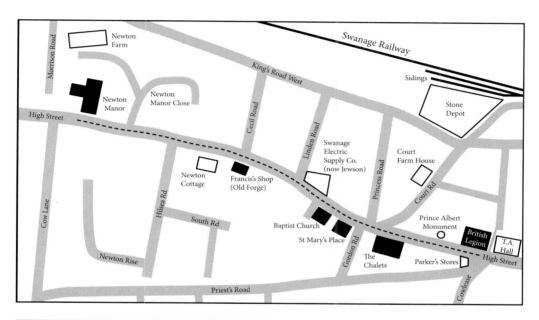

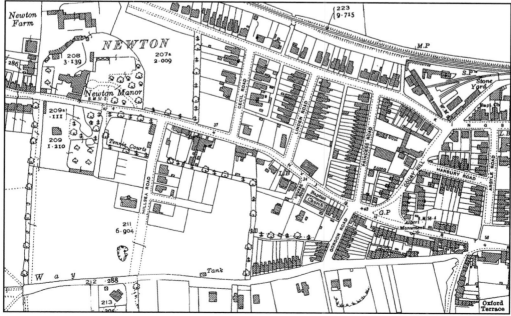

Extract from 1926 OS map.

4.1 Territorial Army Drill Hall, 1930s. The hall was built by government contractors Jesty & Baker of Weymouth and opened by John Ernest Mowlem on 3 December 1933. It had a large room for drill, a recreation room, store, armoury and miniature range. This view shows the local Sea Cadets with their leader Colonel Russell (in the centre). The hall was replaced by Sandringham Court built during 1981/82.

4.2 Opening of the British Legion Club, 3 October 1931. Lord Vivian, brother-in-law of the late Earl Haig, is seen here on the left talking to ex-servicemen who had served in the 'Great War' 1914–18. His rough-haired terrier, 'Raid of Glyn', is just visible in the foreground and as reported in the *Swanage Times* 'not only saw service in France, but took part in a raid and wears his ribbon'.

4.3 Albert the Good Monument, *c*1908. This memorial to Prince Albert was built in 1862 and stood on the High Street above Court Hill. John Mowlem gave the freehold land to the parish, George Burt gave the iron railings, and John and James Haysom cut the inscription. Unfortunately, the Prince's date of birth was incorrectly recorded as 19 August instead of 26 August 1819.

4.4 Albert the Good Monument, August 1971. Developers of the adjoining site took down the monument, causing a public outcry. The author took this photograph during the demolition work. Note wedges in place on the upper courses. The top 13 courses had been removed as unsafe between the two World Wars. The truncated monument has yet to be re-erected elsewhere in Swanage.

4.5 High Street above Court Hill, *c*1905. The old cottage in the centre was built by William Tomes in 1810 and was once one of three cottages on separate plots of land. It was replaced by The Chalets, built to plans dated 1907. The other two cottages survive today. The one seen here on the far left was incorporated into a row of later buildings, and the other, called Stone House, is shown on the next photo.

4.6 Court Hill looking east, *c* 1910. This view can be compared with the one above and shows The Chalets (right) which replaced the central cottage in the previous photo. Stone House mentioned in the last caption is the second building from the right. In the distance is the Albert the Good Monument (see 4.3).

4.7   Court Road, formerly old Gilbert Road, *c* 1912. Court Hill, as it is also known, originally included part of the High Street to the east as far as the Black Swan. John Mowlem was born in one of the old cottages seen here on the left. These were replaced in 1912/13 by the present houses designed by Lionel Way. Osborne Cottages on the right had been built by Fred Pond to plans dated December 1909.

4.8   Court Road and High Street looking west, *c* 1910. The chimney of the old cottage on the left of the last photo is just visible (far right). The row of trees would soon give way to new housing both in Court Road and at the top of Princess Road, when this was eventually connected with the High Street.

4.9   High Street looking west, *c* 1914. On the left are The Chalets and Stone House. Beyond the junction with Gordon Road is St Mary's Place (seen in the next photo). Court Road is on the right. The houses at the top of Princess Road had just been built and the road connected with the High Street (see also 4.11).

4.10 St Mary's Place, High Street, *c* 1915. This row of houses replaced four old cottages, of which the one at the west end W.M. Hardy noted was of 'ancient type', while the 'other three houses were used for the Swanage Poor House' in the early part of the 19th century. The name St Mary's Place is carved over the doorway of the house on the east end, which was for many years the home of the Norman family who are seen here.

4.11   High Street looking east towards Court Hill, *c* 1910. This view is rather difficult to identify today. In 1913 the Swanage Electric Supply Co. built their premises on part of the 'Court Park Estate' on the far left. This building is now Jewson's. Behind the trees in the distance is Princess Road before it was connected with the High Street. The Baptist Church was built during 1920/21 on the land beyond the right of this photo.

4.12 Laying the foundation stone of the Baptist Church, 19 June 1920. Two stones were laid, one by Pastor James Wicks, the other by Beatrice Ellen Beebe in acknowledgement of her generous contributions to the building fund. The church was built by Arthur Bird's firm, whose yard was nearby in Princess Road. The total cost amounted to £2,879 14s 2d, and the new church was opened on 15 May 1921.

4.13 Bill Hancock and his younger brother Arthur in Linden Road, 1920. In the 1930s their father George started a masonry yard in King's Road and took over an old monumental workshop previously owned by Lewis Haysom. Bill and Arthur took over the firm from their father after the Second World War and ran it until their retirement (see 7.7). In the background is the Swanage Electric Supply Co. building (now Jewson).

4.14 Swanage Electric Supply Co. (now Jewson), Linden Road, c 1920. A young 'Mott' Hardy is seen working on the Crossley gas engine used to generate electricity. 'Mott' was later a well-known member of the Swanage Sailing Club. Soon after the Electric Company moved to the gasworks site, the nearby residents sent a petition to the council in 1924 complaining about the noise the gas engine made at night.

4.15 George Francis's shop, High Street, *c* 1930. This is still known as The Old Forge. The building on the far left has a stone inscribed Hatton Cottage. George Francis (seen here) was a furniture dealer and also a 'General Merchant' who bought 'Rag, Iron, Rope, Rubber' and scrap metal. The shop front was later rebuilt (to plans dated 1948), while Hatton Cottage and the warehouse on the right are little changed today.

4.16 Newton Cottage, *c* 1910 (now Heather Close). Built in 1800 by Congregational Minister William Sedcole the cottage was later the home of the Bullen and White families. The author Harold Begbie lived here from 1910–20. Newton Cottage and Res Silenda (a bungalow next door) were destroyed during the air raid of 23 August 1942. Mrs Catherine Jackman and Janet Witt were killed. Retired carpenter Joe Hibbs died later from his injuries.

4.17 High Street looking east from Newton Manor, *c* 1910. On the right are Rumsey and Beaton Cottages, the latter named after Samuel Beaton, owner of Newton Manor from 1830–43. The ruins of these cottages survived for many years before being replaced by new houses in 1980 (on the corner of Hillsea Road).

4.18 Newton Manor, *c* 1920. Dating from the Elizabethan period but much altered, it was the ancestral home of the Cockram family from 1597–1830. In the 1870s the Manor was acquired by Sir John Charles Robinson, Queen Victoria's surveyor of pictures from 1882–1901. The Manor later became a girls' school and is now divided into flats.

Chapter 5
Herston to King's Road West

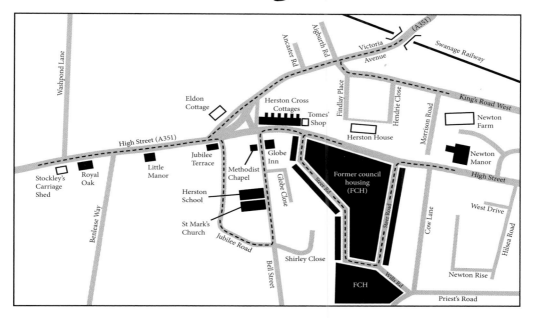

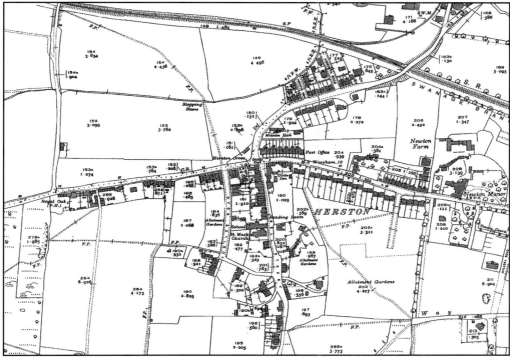

Extract from 1926 OS map.

5.1 Newton Knap, *c* 1905. On the left is Newton Manor. There had once been a Purbeck marble quarry on the right in the grounds of what became Newton Grange. This 1920s building was demolished in 2008 and replaced by a new housing estate called Newton Manor Grange.

5.2 Old Newton Cottages, *c* 1905. By comparing this view with 5.3, it can be seen that the two centre cottages (with the lower roof line) were incorporated into the new row of houses. The house on the corner of what is now Morrison Road has a stone inscribed Newton Place. These houses and the next row became known as Newton Terrace.

5.3 Newton Knap, *c* 1920. The old cottages seen in the previous photo were blended in very well with the new houses either side. The house on the far left is a continuation of Newton Terrace. The house second from the left named Lemnos was built by Burt and Burt to plans dated 14 June 1915.

5.4 High Street looking west, *c* 1923. An early view of the former council houses built in 1920/21. However, Steer Road (named in memory of Rev. Thomas Steer) was not constructed until further council housing was erected during 1927/28. The new road was built by Maidment's of Parkstone (on the far left).

5.5   A. Bird & Co. workers, February 1921. The workforce of A. Bird & Co. pose for a photograph. Arthur Bird had his works in Princess Road and an office on Court Hill (see 6.7). Besides these council houses, another contract that they carried out during 1920/21 was the building of the new Baptist Church (see 4.12).

5.6   Building work in progress, February 1921. After the First World War there was a campaign to provide 'Homes fit for Heroes' and an ex-soldier was chosen as the tenant of the first house completed. Each house had four rooms and a bathroom with a weekly rent of 10s 6d (52½p) per week.

5.7 Steer Road looking north, *c* 1930. More council housing was built during 1927/28, and a tender to build a further 30 houses was accepted from local builders John Parsons & Sons in October 1928. The new road had been laid out by Maidment's of Parkstone who had submitted a tender of £952 8s 6d (£952.42½p) for the work.

5.8 Steer Road looking south, *c* 1930. Steer Road in fact forms a loop back to the High Street. The road was named after Rev. Thomas Steer, Congregational Minister at Swanage from 1880–1908, who was responsible for building the new Congregational Church in 1900–01 (see 2.20). He died at Reading in 1927.

5.9 Herston House, *c* 1908. This 18th century house was purchased by John Mowlem in 1849 for £185. Sadly by the mid 1960s it was derelict and was pulled down in 1967. A stone inscribed 'JM 1850' was reset in the garden wall. The battlements seen here were added by Mowlem and now adorn the garden of Beach Cottage on Shore Road.

5.10 Garden and orchard at the rear of Herston House, *c* 1920. The final residents were retired local photographer George Cox and his wife Laura. Most of Cox's collection of glass plate negatives was unwittingly destroyed when the derelict house was demolished in 1967. A few of these plates are known to have survived.

5.11 View from Herston House looking north to Victoria Avenue, *c* 1925. The gap between the houses on the far right would later form the junction with King's Road West after this was extended to meet Victoria Avenue. The field shown in the foreground is now Findlay Place, most of these houses being built during the 1950s.

5.12 Herston greetings card, *c* 1912. This postcard is a composite of five images of Herston taken around 1904. Each of these photographs is reproduced separately on the following pages. Colour postcards of local views in this composite style are still popular with holiday visitors today.

5.13   Herston Cross Cottages and Tomes's shop in the late 1920s. A postcard view taken by Betha Potter which also shows two horse-drawn stone wagons belonging to The Purbeck Stone & General Trading Co. Ltd. The road was later widened by removing the stone wall and large tree. Herston House was beyond this view on the right.

5.14   Tomes's shop and Post Office, *c* 1931. Frank Tomes took over this shop from Henry Masterman in 1908. Gertrude Tomes seen here (with John Tomes?) took over from her father and ran it until 1953. Harry Tomes succeeded his father in 1956 and had the present shop built in 1960–61. Harry's son and daughter, Keith and Marie took over the business in 2000. From 1958–92 this was the VG Stores (now Costcutter).

In the shade at
HERSTON

5.15 Herston novelty card, *c* 1910. Novelty cards of this type were very fashionable during the Edwardian period. The same card would be overprinted with the name of different seaside resorts. This one seems to show a beach scene, not something you are likely to find at Herston!

5.16 Herston Cross, *c* 1904. Herston Cross Cottages were built in 1899 for John Mowlem Burt by W.M. Hardy's firm at a cost of £3,528. The shop on the end was for many years Barker's and is now The MKL Partnership, Chartered Accountants who have also added a second storey. Herston House can be seen in the distance (see 5.9).

5.17 Herston Cross looking west, *c* 1904. There was a turnpike gate at Herston from 1766 until 1876. George Harris and his wife Barbara were the keepers of the toll gate and retained the post until tolls were abolished (see also 5.34). On the right is Eldon Cottage (seen below).

5.18 Eldon Cottage at Herston Cross in the 1930s. Job Webber (left) with his wife Patience and grandson Robert Blanchard. The cottage had sliding panels in the walls, perhaps dating back to the days of smuggling. Sadly the cottage was demolished to improve the road junction with Victoria Avenue after Mrs Webber died in 1940.

5.19 Bell Street, c 1904. The Globe Inn (left) has been known by this name since at least the mid 18th century, long before George Burt's 'Great Globe'. The pub was run by the Bower family for many years, starting with Robert Bower who took over from Henry Bendell in 1911, then Robert's widow Alice until she died in 1945, followed by her son Cyril. He was succeeded by his son Michael in 1983, who ran the pub until 1996.

5.20 Methodist Chapel, Bell Street, c 1910. The Wesleyan Ebenezer Chapel was built in 1861 and, apart from the loss of the railings, looks little changed today. In 2009 it became the Girlguiding Swanage District HQ. Bell Street was named after Rev. Andrew Bell, Rector of Swanage from 1801–09. It had also been known as West Street.

5.21 Linington's shop, Bell Street, *c* 1909. Harry Linington was a grocer and confectioner who also had a shop in the High Street at Swanage. This postcard was sent at 8.45 am on 20 October 1909 to Tom Linington on his birthday by his cousin Molly and would have arrived the same day. The shop building was known as Bridle (or Bridal) House (seen below).

5.22 Co-operative Society shop, Bell Street, 1920s. This was 'No. 10 Branch' of the Parkstone & Bournemouth Co-operative Society. They also had a shop in Swanage at York Buildings (near the Town Hall). In addition to branches in the Bournemouth area, they had shops at Poole, Christchurch, Wimborne and Blandford. Outside the shop is Claud King (left) with an assistant. In the 1934 *Swanage Street Directory* grocer George Weekes is listed here and also at 343 High Street, the 'Herston Grocery and Provision Stores'. More recently the building seen here has been converted to residential use.

5.23 Herston School, Bell Street, *c* 1910. Some of the children are wearing medals awarded for regular attendance. On the right is James Butler, Headmaster of the school for 39 years until his retirement in 1945. Mr Butler had previously held teaching posts in Weymouth and London, but this was his only headmastership.

5.24 'School's out', Bell Street, July 1901. An infants school in Bell Street, seen here further up the street on the right, had originally been built in 1855 through the efforts of the new rector Rev. Robert Duncan Travers. Mrs Frances Serrell of Langton gave the land and local quarrymen the stone. It was extended in 1865 to accommodate older children, with further extensions in 1871, 1888 and 1914.

5.25 St Mark's Church, Bell Street, looking north, *c* 1904. St Mark's Church (left) was begun in 1869 and cost £1,400 to build. It was designed by John Hicks of Dorchester who employed the young Thomas Hardy before he became a full-time novelist. The single church bell was cast in 1871 by John Warner & Sons of Cripplegate, London. Due to a shortage of funds the church was not completed and consecrated until 25 April 1872.

5.26 Bell Street looking north, *c* 1904. On the far right is a stable, forming part of a mineral water factory built by John King of Rothelstone House in 1884. By 1896 it had been taken over by Denning's of Weymouth and in turn by the South Western Mineral Water Company *c* 1901. The business moved to Kings Road in 1907. Council housing was built on the site of the factory in Bell Street during the early 1960s.

5.27 Bell Street, *c* 1875. An early view showing where Jubilee Road now meets Bell Street. Victoria Terrace on the left still remains, but the old houses on the right were apparently dismantled by Fred Keats (during evenings) in the 1930s. New housing was built on this site during 2009/10.

5.28 Jubilee Road, 1914. The new extension to Herston School seen here was built in this year. In the distance is the gasometer which survived until about 1980. On this postcard sent by a soldier named 'Bobby' to 'F. Southey Esq' of Warminster on 20 December 1914, he says, 'this is a view of our camp, if you look long enough you will see it in the distance! Still further off are the huts, they are not quite as far on as they look in the photo'.

5.29 High Street looking east, *c* 1912. On the far left is Eldon Cottage, formerly the home of the Corben family and latterly Job and Patience Webber. In the centre are Herston Cross Cottages and to the right Providence Terrace, Jubilee Road and Jubilee Terrace. The last two were named in honour of Queen Victoria's Golden Jubilee in 1887. Note the advertising board for the Central Garage in Station Road.

5.30 Grocer's shop on the corner of Jubilee Road, *c* 1909. Henry Arnum Masterman had been a shoemaker here at Jubilee Terrace from the late 1880s before becoming the sub-postmaster. He later moved to Herston Cross Cottages and this shop was taken over by George Vye who had previously been licensee at the Globe Inn in Bell Street from 1902–09. In the 1930s the shop was run by Ernest Masters and Miss Lucy Masters. However, it no longer sells grocery or sweets and is now Harlee's Fish and Chips.

5.31 High Street looking east, *c* 1925. Apart from the width of the main road this view has changed very little. The 'high pavement' on the right still exists, although wooden railings and a grass bank now protect pedestrians from the steep drop to the road. This can be compared with photo 5.41, a later view showing the other side of the road.

5.32 Little Manor, *c* 1960. This interesting house has a stone inscribed 'Laurel Villa' on the right hand corner of the front wall. For many years it was the home of the Stevens family. Tom Stevens, who died in 1945, drove the horse-drawn Mail Coach between Swanage and Wareham. He was also a 'Charabanc and Brake Proprietor' and in 1909 advertised trips to Corfe Castle and Studland in his 'Pride of Purbeck' and 'Surprise' horse-drawn charabancs.

5.33 The Royal Oak, High Street, looking east, *c* 1920. The buildings on the right are probably late 18th or early 19th century. The Royal Oak pub does not appear by name in trade directories until 1859 when Thomas Stevens was the licensee, although it had been a pub or 'beer shop' from at least the early 1830s. The Haysom family kept the pub from 1885–1906 and the Honess family from 1913–35.

5.34 Harris's shop, High Street, *c* 1905. George Harris opened a grocer's shop here in the 1880s which was carried on by his widow Barbara who died in 1916. The *Swanage & Wareham Guardian* noted that 'she supported herself and her son and daughter (till they married) by working up a little general business, and many of her poorer neighbours have been helped in times of need by her generosity' (see also 5.17). In the 1930s the shop was run by Arthur Draper. It can also be seen in the background of the photo 5.36.

5.35 Houses on the corner of Belle Vue Lane, 1965. A rare view showing these buildings shortly before demolition. The shop in the next photo can be seen on the right. The cottages on the far left still remain, adjoining what is now called Benlease Way.

5.36 High Street looking east, 1969. The buildings in the last photo have been demolished and Herston Stores seen here would soon be replaced by a new house. The shop sign says 'Grocer, Provision Merchant, Cigarettes, Confectionery, etc.' Some of the cottages on the left probably date from the 18th century and are faced with high-quality ashlar squared masonry, suggesting it was surplus from a major job elsewhere.

5.37 Royal Fusiliers, High Street, looking east, 1912. The advance party from the London Regiment of the Royal Fusiliers march to one of the summer volunteer camps which were held at Whitecliff and Herston most years up until the start of the First World War. The buildings on the right were a stable and carriage shed built for Albert Stockley in 1903, which survived until recent years when the adjoining cottage was restored. This cottage and the outbuildings can also be seen behind the tents in the next view.

5.38 7th Worcesters Regiment Camp, August 1908. There were between 5000 and 6000 Territorials in Swanage for the camps that summer. The 7th Worcesters comprised 20 officers, 94 non-commissioned officers and 593 men, totalling 707. This postcard was sent by a soldier named 'Bert' to a 'Miss Lizzie Arnold' of Kidderminster. The camp site is now the Swanage Middle School playing field.

5.39 Albert Stockley, driver of the Royal Mail cart, *c* 1906. This view was taken by his carriage shed (see 5.37). Albert was the driver of the mail cart for several years from 1906 and owned a horse-drawn carriage, plying for hire to summer visitors on the seafront. He was listed in the 1916 *Swanage Street Directory* as a 'carriage proprietor'. He also helped coal the paddle steamer *Monarch* on her first trip to Swanage in 1888. From the 1890s until the period of the First World War he was a fishmonger and toured Purbeck as both a fish salesman and market gardener. Albert was also an enthusiastic exhibitor at the local horticultural show, winning many cups and prizes.

5.40 Royal Mail cart, High Street, looking west, *c* 1906. The cart is positioned across the main road to Wareham and to the left of Albert Stockley's stable and carriage shed. Note the Royal Cypher for King Edward VII on the side of the mail cart.

5.41 High Street looking east, *c* 1930. Retracing our steps from the Royal Oak, this view shows the main road before it was widened and Eldon Cottage demolished to improve the road junction with Victoria Avenue. Eldon Cottage was one of the few remaining thatched buildings in Swanage and home of the Webber family until 1940 (see 5.18).

5.42 Victoria Avenue, *c* 1912. Before going down what is now King's Road West, this is a view looking back to Herston from the railway bridge. Only a few houses had been built on Victoria Avenue, while most of those on the right of the photo date from the 1920s. Herston Cross Cottages are visible in the middle distance (see 5.16).

5.43 William Steele, Newton Farm, *c* 1930. Another view that is difficult to place today. In the background are the wooden railings seen in the previous photo. The track would later be joined to the existing section of King's Road West which ended level with Newton Manor and Newton Farm (see 1926 OS map overleaf).

5.44 William Steele, Newton Farm, *c* 1910. The farm was apparently supplied like a 'kit-of-parts' and built by the mid 1870s. The Morrison family from Scotland took it over in 1899/1900. When John Morrison died in 1920 the *Swanage Times* noted, 'he made his land his study and got good crops'. After Mrs Maggie Morrison died in 1937 the farm was demolished for housing and a new road built, called appropriately Morrison Road.

Chapter 6
King's Road West and Court Road

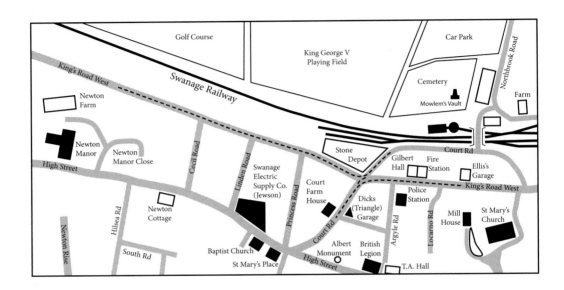

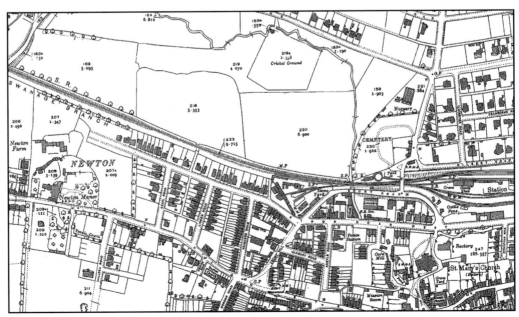

Extract from 1926 OS map.

6.1 King's Road West, *c* 1914. The row of houses on the left (now Nos 79–85) were built to plans dated March 1912 together with Nos 1–9 Princess Road. Most of the other houses further along this part of King's Road were built during the Edwardian period. The row of trees in the distance marked the end of the road at that time, level with Newton Manor and Newton Farm.

6.2 Princess Road, *c* 1914. The houses on the right (Nos 2–34) were built in stages to plans dated 1904–06. The plans for Nos 1–9 on the left are dated March 1912. This road was originally a cul-de-sac and the connection with the High Street was not made until the building of the row of houses Nos 36–50, seen in the distance on the right.

6.3 Fred Haysome, 'Fly Proprietor', Court Road, _c_ 1910. Like many 'fly' and horse-drawn cab proprietors, Fred Haysome would soon be servicing motor cars. This building was largely demolished in 1979/80. Stone stacked in Burt and Burt's yard is seen on the left. This later became Haysom & Sons stone depot. It is now divided into the Kings Court Business Centre and Swanage Town Council Depot.

6.4 Haysom & Sons stone depot, King's Road, _c_ 1930. Back row (L to R): Sam Florence, Fred Lock, Fred Haysom, Phil Brown. Middle row: Walter Haysom, Bert Tomes, Albert Phippard, Arthur Bonfield, John Haysom, Jimmy Chinchen, Harry Phippard, Bert Norman. Front row: Frank Haysom, Harry Gillingham, Harold Haysom, Charlie Coleman, Harry Tomes, Teddy Corben, Arthur Corben, Sid Cooper.

6.5 Swanage Fire Brigade at the junction of King's Road and Court Road, *c* 1920.
Back row (L to R): John King (driver), Fred Bennett, Fred Moss, Arthur Summers. Front
row: Harry Gallop, Harry Chinchen, William Vaughan, Thomas Day, Capt. Alister Lloyd,
Freeland White, Frank Bishop, James Goater, William Chinchen, Reg Goater.

6.6 Court Farm House, *c* 1910. This was part of Carents Court and a working farm until
1900. The Court landholding is documented back to the 12th century and was more than
400 acres. It was gradually sold off until only the farmhouse remained, refurbished to its
present state in about 1850. Carents Court has passed through the hands of Carent, Malet,
Walrond, Bond, Frampton, Gould, Rose, Chapman, Dampier and Burt.

6.7 William Hicks outside his builder's office, Court Road, c 1924. William Hicks from Bath came to Swanage in 1920 as the foreman for Arthur Bird's building firm and was in charge of building the new Baptist Church. The building seen here was the firm's office built in that same year. William started his own business in 1924. He was apparently colour blind and this resulted in some odd combinations of colours being used for the interior decoration of his own house Ivydene (next door). This office was later used as a shoemaker's shop and was replaced by a new house in 1980.

6.8 Ivydene, Court Road, c 1946. The Hicks family renamed the former Court Farm House as Ivydene. Seen here are William Hicks and his wife Clara. The building next door was used by Mr Hicks as his builder's office (shown above). Note the concrete-roofed brick air raid shelter at the top of Court Hill, which was converted into public toilets. The Chalets in the High Street beyond can also be seen (see 4.6).

6.9 Kingdom Hall of the Jehovah's Witnesses, Court Road, 2010. A modern image. This was formerly Dicks & Son's Triangle Garage and later the cycle shop Two Wheels. The first garage was built here by Arthur Garman in the early 1920s and was enlarged by Ernest Dicks to plans dated 1929. The petrol pump plinths are still visible either side of the door. The garage covered the old Court Pond so a drinking trough had to be provided (this was later covered up). Court Hill Wines can be seen on the left (see 6.10).

6.10 Tom Bending's sweet shop and tobacconists, Court Road, _c_ 1980. This shop was originally built for grocer and fruiterer Fred Loader to plans dated 1905. By 1920 it was a fish and chip shop run by Walter King, who also had a stall at the market in Station Road next to the Swanage Cinema. This view was taken when the shop was up for sale after Tom Bending's retirement. Today it is Court Hill Wines.

6.11 Swanage Fire Brigade at the corner of Argyle Road, 1907. Their new Merryweather 'Greenwich Gem'-type steam fire engine was aptly named *The Swan* and replaced a small manual fire engine given to the town by George Burt in December 1874. The first call out of the new engine was to a rick fire at nearby Court Pond and took 'the much improved time of 13 minutes to get there from the first ring of the fire bell'.

6.12 Swanage Fire Brigade, Nichols & Son's Garage, King's Road, 1907. The brigade arranged with garage proprietor Henry Nichols to keep the new steam fire engine here. The fire brigade would later occupy other premises before this building officially became the Fire Station from July 1930. It was superseded in 1975 by the present station further along King's Road, opposite the Parish Church.

6.13   Gilbert Hall, King's Road, 13 May 1910. This hall and the adjoining garage (seen in the previous photo) had been built by local builders H. & J. Hardy in 1906. The hall was used for a variety of events and entertainments. Here are the cast of the Swanage Lyric Society's production of *The Mandarin*, 'a Chinese Musical Operetta' by Edmonds & West.

6.14 Inside the Gilbert Hall, May 1910. This is a rare interior view showing the set for *The Mandarin*. It became the Church Hall from 1920 until it was sold in the mid 1970s. The building was last used around 1990 for a dinosaur exhibition featuring 'Iggy' the iguanodon (made by one of the local schools) who stood 15 ft high and 30 ft long. The hall was demolished in December 2003 and has been replaced by Chestnut Mews.

Gilbert Hall Cinema,

KING'S ROAD, SWANAGE.

(TWO MINUTES FROM STATION).

Up=to=Date Pictures well shown.

OPEN ALL THE YEAR ROUND at 8 p.m.

Entire Change of Programme Three Times Weekly:
Monday, Wednesday and Friday.

6.15 Gilbert Hall advertisement, *c* 1914. The cinema was 'Two Minutes From Station' but in the advert on the next page it had become '3 Minutes'! These were the days of not only silent films but also the use of highly inflammable nitrate film. In 1915 there was a report of a fire in the projection box (sited in the gallery). Troops attending the film raised the alarm, but the fire was extinguished before the fire brigade arrived.

6.16 Gilbert Hall advertisement, 1917. The Million Dollar Girls were appearing at the Gilbert Hall during the summer of 1917. This was the first season after the cinema had been moved from here to the newly built Electric Theatre in Station Road. In addition to films and shows the hall had been used for the then-popular roller skating craze; admission (in 1910) was 6d (2½p) during the day, 3d (1p) in the evenings, with skate hire costing 6d (2½p).

6.17 **The Swanage Electric Cinema, 1915.** Films had previously been shown at the Central Hall in Station Road (for a few months) before the Gilbert Hall was used as a more permanent cinema from May 1912. The film advertised here was the 1912 Italian silent version of *Quo Vadis?* Until 1915 this cinema had been known as the Gilbert Hall Pictures. It closed when the new purpose-built Electric Theatre opened in Station Road in June 1916 (see 7.41).

6.18 **Staff of the Swanage Electric Cinema, *c* 1915.** Back row (L to R): Charlie Linington, Frankie Parker, Tom Sidnell (manager), Gerry Stockley, Freddie Cooper. Front row: Bert Bradford(?), unknown, Edward Stockley. Some of the staff, including the manager Tom Sidnell and projectionist Gerry Stockley, transferred to the new Electric Theatre in Station Road, together with the hand-cranked projection equipment previously set up in the hall gallery.

6.19 Swanage Fire Station, King's Road, *c* 1932. This unusual fire engine was converted from an old Daimler car obtained from Haysome's Garage. After the present Fire Station was built the old station was used again during repairs to the new fire station floor. It was eventually demolished in January 2004 a few weeks after the adjoining Church Hall. The shop on the left was run in the 1930s by greengrocer Tom Purchase.

6.20 O.F. Stevens' garage, King's Road, *c* 1914. Messrs Usher and Webber pose for the camera. Wareham-based motor engineer Owen Stevens took over this garage from Nichols & Son in 1913. He also ran a charabanc service to Wareham and Studland using green 34 hp Commer Cars. During 1916–17 the garage was used by G. Owen Ellis (see 6.24) and in 1919–20 by John T. Dickings (see 1.52).

6.21 Overland Cars advertisement, *c* 1914. O.F. Stevens was the sole agent in Dorset for American-made Overland cars. In 1914 the 'Torpedo' touring car cost £275 and was 'Absolutely the Last Thing in Refinement' with a 'Handsome 5-seater Body, Hood, Screen, all Lamps, Speedometer' and they offered 'Immediate Delivery'. The firm was best known for the design and production of the Jeep during the Second World War.

6.22 Swanage Fire Station, King's Road *c* 1940. The station is sandbagged and ready for action, with Freddie Summers 'on duty'. During the Second World War the local fire brigade became part of the Auxiliary Fire Service, which in 1941 merged with the regular Fire Brigades to become the National Fire Service. The firemen in Swanage were kept busy dealing with fires often started by incendiary bombs dropped during air raids.

6.23 Swanage Steam Laundry, King's Road, *c* 1932. This also shows the fire engine converted from a Daimler car by the fire brigade (see 6.19). The Laundry was built to plans dated 1901. These premises were later used by local builder Jefferson Pond. Swanbrook Mews was built on the site by Turner & Wright Ltd during 1987/88.

6.24 G. Owen Ellis's Millmead Motor Works, King's Road, 1931. Glyndwr Owen Ellis (seen on the left) initially took over the right-hand workshop from local builder Job Hardy in 1923, followed by the other one from 1931. In 1938 'Glyn' Owen Ellis had a new garage built on this site, which after his retirement was taken over and altered in 1948 by the Southern National Bus Company (later Western National). In January 1974 it was taken over by Hants & Dorset (now Wilts & Dorset) and is still in use today.

6.25 Swanage Liberal Club outing, July 1919. This photo of Royal Blue charabanc No. 5 was taken by the Parish Church in King's Road. Note the solid tyres on this new AEC YC vehicle of 1919. The Royal Blue business started in Bournemouth in 1880 and purchased their first motor charabanc in 1913. The Liberal Club Hall in Chapel Lane (built in 1913) was destroyed during the air raid on 3 February 1943 (see 2.8).

6.26 Swanage Fire Brigade in King's Road, 1931. This was their first motor fire engine purchased in 1925 and called *White Rose*. It was named in honour of Chief Officer Gideon White who had served with the brigade for 34 years. Back row (L to R): E. Langdon, P. Foot, F. White, R. Hoptroff, H. Chinchen, B. Matthews. Front row: S. Pitcher, H. Goodchild, F. Stockley, H. Gallop, W. Vaughan, Chief Officer C.A. Colmer. This fire engine was later fitted with pneumatic tyres.

7.0   Aerial view, 1926. In the foreground is the Royal Victoria Hotel, showing the lawn and garden at the front. The Parade and Mowlem Institute are in the centre, with Station Road and the Railway Station beyond. The extensive carriage and goods sidings in the Station Yard can be seen where the Health Centre and supermarket are today. The long building just below this is the old Drill Hall (behind the Conservative Club). This photograph can be compared with the 1926 OS map opposite. (Photograph courtesy of Purbeck Press.)

Chapter 7
St Mary's Church to The Parade

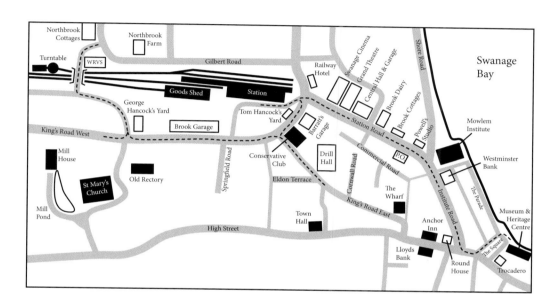

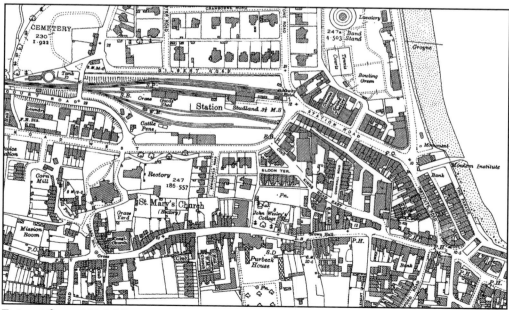

Extract from 1926 OS map.

7.1 St Mary's Parish Church during the flood on 17 November 1935. This composite image shows the extent of the flooding. The *Swanage Times* reported that religious services were cancelled and all efforts concentrated on rendering aid to those in distress. The most recent flood to affect this part of Swanage occurred on 3 February 1990, hopefully the like of which will not be seen again since the implementation of an extensive flood relief scheme.

7.2 The Old Rectory, King's Road, *c* 1930. The south-east section was probably built in the 16th century, the centre section in the 18th century, and the part on the left during the 19th century. The house was sold at auction in June 1927 to Joseph Parsons for £2,500 and became the Parsons family home (in 1921 he also bought the Mill House and Mill Pond). The Rectory was moved to Cranborne Road and again some years after the War to Church Hill. The row of tall trees, like many others in Swanage, has now gone.

7.3 Station Yard, 19 July 1938. In the background is George Hancock's stone yard (see 7.7). The locomotive shunting wagons in the yard is an Adams T1 class tank No. 7, built in 1894 and withdrawn in 1951. The fireman appears to be catching up with his reading between the shunting operations!

7.4 Swanage Station during the flood on 17 November 1935. It was reported that the flood water rose above the axle boxes of the rolling stock. This scene was repeated on 3 February 1990, when some enterprising Swanage Railway volunteers manned a small dinghy from the main platform to go up the line. The water soon receded but not without damaging the electrics of the signalling system.

7.5 Cottages at Northbrook looking north, *c* 1930. An unusual view from Northbrook Bridge showing the old cottage adjoining the railway line. This was later replaced by the WRVS headquarters and has more recently been converted to residential use. The row of cottages in the background are shown in more detail in the next photograph.

7.6 Northbrook Cottages, September 1968. These old cottages were replaced by the housing development called Gilbert Court (built to plans dated April 1971). The author was told some years ago that the cottages were in the process of being reroofed on the day the *Titanic* sank, 15 April 1912.

7.7 George Hancock & Sons, 'Quarry Owners & Masons', King's Road, 1968. George Hancock took over an old monumental workshop from Lewis Haysom in 1931/32. The yard seen here was on the corner of King's Road and Court Road, opposite the Parish Church. After the Second World War George's sons Bill and Arthur carried on the business until their retirement. The Fire Station now occupies this site.

7.8 Brook Garage, King's Road, *c* 1960. The original garage was built by Frank Holmes and opened in August 1926. After this view was taken various alterations were made to the garage including the provision of a canopy. In 1993 plans were submitted by Lo-Cost Stores Ltd to demolish the garage and erect a new supermarket, which is currently called 'The co-operative food'.

7.9 Springfield Road during the flood on 17 November 1935. This view gives a good idea of the depth of water on that occasion. The houses on the right were built in the 1920s. In the foreground is a sign for George Hancock's masonry yard which supplied 'garden ornaments, paving, rockery, etc.'

7.10 Springfield Road after the air raid of 14 May 1941. This was the first raid to cause serious damage in Swanage and included the bombing of Wesley's Cottage in the High Street. There were no fatalities in the raid, but 19 people were injured. Note Charles Wilson's removal van in use during the clearing up operations.

7.11 King's Road, *c* 1920. A local group on an outing to Bournemouth in the Swanage Motor Company's 1917 Darracq 14-seater wagonette (left) and 1919 Lacre 30-seater charabanc (with solid tyres). The Swanage Motor Company was started by Messrs Ruthven and Jackson who had a garage built in the lower High Street in 1919 (later Dean & Son, see 1.18). They also ran the Turk's Head Hotel Garage in Lincoln.

7.12 Swanage Conservative Club, King's Road, *c* 1912. This distinctive building was designed by Lionel Way and erected by local builder Fred Pond on land given by the Earl of Eldon. It opened officially on 5 October 1911. Previously the Club premises were in King's Road East and it had been known as the Constitutional Club (formed in 1883).

7.13 Dean & Barratt's Station Garage, *c* **1930.** The Post Office now occupies this site. To the right is the Conservative Club. In 1928 Reginald Dean and Richard Barratt took over the garage from well-known local businessman Russell Parsons. The Dean & Barratt partnership ended in 1932 when it became Barratts of Swanage.

7.14 Dean & Barratt's Station Garage, *c* **1930.** Neville & Co.'s 'Ladies Wear Salons' were at the front of the garage entrance. On the right is a sign for the 'The Green Cars'. These motor coaches provided tours to the 'Beauty Spots of Dorset, Devon, Somerset, Wilts & Hants'. Dean & Barratt also had the Swanage Motor Works in lower High Street (later Dean & Son's 'The Swanage Garages', see 1.18).

7.15 Barratts of Swanage Station Garage during the flood on 17 November 1935. This view of King's Road also shows the Conservative Club. On the right are the coal order offices of H.W. Beavis and J.W. Burt. The flood on 3 February 1990 also reached this point but did not affect Station Road as it did in 1914 and 1935 (see 7.51 and 7.62).

7.16 Barratt's showroom shortly before demolition, *c* 1970. Plans for the new Post Office were submitted in March 1970 and involved the demolition of this showroom and the old garage at the back, originally the Drill Hall (see following photos). The main contractor for the new Post Office was Burt & Vick of Poole and it was opened officially by Council Chairman Harry Smith on 14 February 1974.

7.17 View from the Town Hall looking north to King's Road East, mid 1960s. This shows the Railway Station and Conservative Club on the left. In the centre is the old Drill Hall used as a garage by Barratts of Swanage. The postal sorting office is now on this site. On the right is Hayter's builders yard (later Queensbury Contractors), demolished in March 2007 and replaced by housing called The Yard.

7.18 Drill Hall, King's Road East, September 1970. The Drill Hall was built in 1886 for the local Volunteer Company of the Royal Garrison Artillery on land owned by Lord Eldon. They trained using guns at Peveril Point and in 1905 won the King's Prize competition held at Shoeburyness. The King's Cup was presented to them personally by King Edward VII. The company was disbanded in April 1922 as the younger men in Swanage who served in the 'Great War' were 'fed up with war'.

7.19 Demolition of the old Drill Hall, King's Road East, *c* 1970. This photo was taken soon after the previous one. After the Volunteer Company was disbanded in 1922, local businessman Russell Parsons used this corrugated iron structure as a garage. The unusual car seen here is a rare Ford Special which had a fibreglass body shell. This particular vehicle still exists and in 2010 was being restored to running order.

7.20 King's Road East during the flood of 1964. Efforts were made to build a dam to divert flood water back into the Brook. This flood scene was repeated on 9 March 1981 when concrete blocks for the new Health Centre, then under construction, were used to form a similar barrier.

7.21 King's Road during the flood on 14 September 1962. The flood water did not stop the lorry or the Hants & Dorset bus Bristol LL6B (registration KEL 404). This bus was new in June 1959 and had been modified at the rear (to prevent grounding) for use on the Sandbanks Ferry service only a month before this view was taken. It was withdrawn in 1969 and sold to a school at High Wycombe in September 1971.

7.22   Tom Hancock's masonry yard, King's Road, *c* 1970. Tom Hancock took over two pieces of land and an office from coal merchant J.W. Burt in 1937. The workshops seen here were cleared away in the 1970s and the area designated a 'green lung' or public open space. Extensive piling work was necessary when the new Health Centre was built on part of this site.

7.23 Tom Hancock's masonry yard, King's Road, *c* 1950. Jimmy Chinchen (left) is seen chatting to Hants & Dorset bus driver Bill Turnock. After the railway opened in 1885 the station yard was used for storing worked stone, and the 'bankers' or stone yards were cleared away from the seafront. Stone was then transported by rail rather than sea. In the 1920s the short-lived Dorset Quarry Company built a loading ramp and erected a crane in the station yard, which can be seen in aerial view 7.0.

7.24 Jimmy Chinchen (left) and Alban Rose at Tom Hancock's yard in the 1950s. They are checking a piece of dressed stone with a template. Jimmy started work in his father's quarry at the age of 13 in August 1901 and retired nearly 70 years later at Christmas 1969. His memories of underground quarrying and the stone trade were recorded on tape by local historian John Dean in May 1971. The tape also included the recollections of stonemason Ralph Bower.

7.25 Swanage Station in the 1930s. The branch line from Wareham opened in May 1885 with stations at Corfe Castle and Swanage. After numerous complaints about the short platform canopy at Swanage the Southern Railway finally provided a new canopy and extended the station buildings during 1937/38. Corfe Castle station remains virtually as built, although the station master's house is on the right-hand end.

7.26 Swanage Station in the mid 1960s. This view can be compared with the above photo which shows the station buildings before they were extended. The Benn and Cronin indicator board on the right was retained and gave a summary of train times and destinations. Apart from the removal of this board the station looks little changed today. Swanage Railway now share the building with the Wilts & Dorset Bus Company and Swanage Associated Taxis.

7.27 Town Band on the station forecourt, 1900. The first Town Band was formed in 1862 when a number of young men got together and purchased instruments. The present Town Band was formed in 1995. They meet every week at the Town Hall and perform regularly at local events. The Railway Hotel (built in 1886) was originally going to be named the Mowlem Hotel. It closed in 1981.

7.28 Cycle corps on the station forecourt, *c* 1908. This view looking towards Station Road shows the cycle corps from one of the summer volunteer/territorial camps held at Swanage before the First World War. The row of shops seen in the centre was extended in 1914 and the bust of Milton (seen here in the end wall) was removed. However, a bust of Shakespeare can still be seen on the other end (at the entrance to Commercial Road).

7.29   Troops and horses on the station forecourt, *c* 1915. Troops are mustered at the station with their horses and gun carriages. Throughout the First World War the Swanage area was used extensively for training and permanent hutted camps were built at Ulwell and 'New Swanage'. Railway wagons (right) were loaded with hay, in the days when fodder for the horses was essential, before the army became more mechanised.

7.30 Troops on station platform, *c* 1918. A familiar scene during the First World War as troops possibly on their way to 'the front' bid farewell to their loved ones. After the War the majority of the huts at the army camps in Swanage were sold and dismantled to be used elsewhere. However, one camp was converted to housing and became The Sunshine Estate (now Ballard Estate).

7.31 Swanage Railway Home Guard during the Second World War. Among the group on the Universal Carrier Mk 1 or 'Bren Gun Carrier' are chief booking clerk Dicky Daw (in the driving seat) and station master G. Nobbs (far left). Two 'regulars', a sergeant and corporal, are standing on the right. Note the station name has been removed in case of invasion. Road signs were also removed to confuse the enemy.

7.32 'Salute the Soldier Week', 1–8 July 1944. Fundraising on the 'home front' was an important part of the war effort. L to R: ganger Edwin Bird, driver Charlie Boyland, signalman Wilf Ford, bookstall manageress Phyllis Cook, Col. Seldon from Salisbury, unknown army officer and Dorchester-based cleaner Stan Brown.

7.33 Swanage Station, 13 May 1962. 'M7' class No. 30379 waits at the main platform with the branch train to Wareham. The last members of this class of locomotives were withdrawn in 1964 and scrapped apart from Nos 30145 and 30053 which were preserved. After spending many years as a static exhibit at Steamtown, Vermont, USA, No. 30053 was repatriated and following restoration can now be seen on the Swanage Railway.

7.34 Swanage Station, September 1969. By this time the goods yard had been closed and the track lifted. The run-round loop and bay platform track had also been removed and only a single line remained into the main platform. There were still busy days, as this excursion train shows; however, closure had already been proposed. The last train ran on Saturday 1 January 1972 and the line was closed officially 2 days later.

7.35 and 7.36 Swanage Station, summer 1972. As soon as the statutory 6 months had elapsed after closure the remaining track was quickly removed. The author took this view and the one below during track-lifting operations. The track has already gone and the rail chairs (that held the track) are being loaded onto a lorry using a mechanical excavator. (Reproduced from old slides)

7.37 Station Road, *c* 1925. On the far left are the builders office of Pond & Walton and J.S. Date's estate agency (the shed next to it). Between this and the Swanage Cinema (now Budgens) was an open-air market. Next to the cinema was the Grand Theatre and Central Garage. The Swanage Gas Company's offices are on the far right. The buildings on this corner were destroyed in the air raid on 20 April 1942.

7.38   Coombes' shop, Station Road, *c* 1922. This was to the left of the Swanage Cinema (now Budgens). It was run by Ernest Yeatman Coombes and his wife Florence May (seen here). The board says 'Draper, Tea and Fancy Goods Dealer'. The shop closed when he bought a Trojan delivery van.

7.39 Station Road at the time of the Silver Jubilee in May 1935. The row of shops to the left from Plummers the House Agents (now Corben & Son) to Commercial Road was built by George Burt in 1893 (the date can be seen on the drainpipes). The shops on the right were built in 1914. Hunt's the grocers was run by William Dunesby. Strong's Café took over these premises from Owen Hardy's wireless shop. Eddie Strong is seen by the van.

7.40 Swanage Gas Company's offices, Station Road, *c* 1920. This view was taken by local photographer George Cox and was printed from a broken glass plate negative rescued from Cox's former home at Herston House during demolition in 1967. Sadly the majority of his collection of old Swanage negatives was unwittingly destroyed.

7.41 Swanage Cinema, Station Road, April 1930. This was built by George Pond and opened in June 1916 as the Electric Theatre. The opening was rushed to accommodate the Royal Welch Fusiliers stationed in the town at the time. The cinema was converted to a two-storey building in 1922 by local builders Pond & Walton who added a balcony and renamed it the Swanage Cinema. L to R: Gerry Stockley (chief projectionist), Dick Mayo (second operator), George Holmes (rewind boy). In April 1953 the cinema was taken over by Tony Whitehouse and renamed the Ritz, which he closed in October 1959 and turned into a supermarket (now Budgens).

7.42   **Swanage Cinema advertisement, *c* 1923.** The 1920s was the era of silent film epics.

7.43 *Swanage Cinegoers Guide*, June 1930. The cinema was equipped to show sound films in March 1930, although some silent films were still shown. Many of the early sound films used the 'sound-on-disc' system on phonograph records which could become out of synchronisation with the actual picture, particularly if the film reels had been damaged. The programme for June 1930 included Al Jolson in *Say it With Songs* and Buster Keaton in the silent film *Spite Marriage* which according to the *Sunday News* 'will make even a Scotsman who paid for his seat laugh!'.

7.44 Queues for the Cinema in the 1930s. Such a queue as this on a rainy afternoon in August was not unusual when 'going to the pictures' provided the main form of mass entertainment. Dick Mayo, former manager of both cinemas, recalled that 'in the summer we had queues past the Railway Hotel and the other way round into Mermond Place.'

7.45   Swanage Pavilion Ltd, Station Road, *c* 1920. London-based comedian Freddy Beck (seen here on the left) had been putting on 'entertainments' in Swanage for 9 years, initially at the Promenade Pavilion on Shore Road (formerly the concert pitch) and later at the Mowlem Institute. This view shows a new entrance being added to these former army huts which had recently been erected on this site.

7.46 The 'Casino', Swanage Pavilion Ltd, *c* 1922. Freddy Beck's 'Casino' after further alterations, when he was presenting his own show *Ye Olde Royalists*. The manager was Randolph King who came from London, and one of the performers was a young Betty Tunnell. The shops either side of the entrance sold chocolates and cooked meats. The 'Casino' later became the Grand Theatre, opened on 9 June 1924.

7.47 Looking towards the Station, *c* 1924. The Central Garage is on the far right and next to this the Grand Theatre and the Swanage Cinema (both now part of Budgens). The unusual three-wheeled car on the left was built by Owen Hardy and is parked near his shop the Swanage Wireless Depot. The shop seen on the far left is now Jill Blanchard's New and Secondhand Bookshop.

7.48 Tom Sherbourne's Entertainers at the Grand Theatre, 1931. 'The smartest concert party that has ever appeared in Swanage.' The daily summer evening performances included singing, dancing, comedy, ventriloquism and revues. Matinees were given on 'Wednesdays, Saturdays and all wet days'. Prices: 'Orchestra Stalls 3s 6d (17½p), Stalls 2s 4d (11½p), Back Stalls 1s 10d (9p), Unreserved Seats 1s 3d (6p)'.

7.49 The Alhambra Rink, Station Road, *c* 1920. This was above the Central Garage (later Woolworths) and was run by Frankie Parker. It opened on 8 December 1919 for roller skating and dancing and held a regular Fancy Dress Skating Carnival (seen here) with admission for skaters 1s 3d (6p) and spectators 5d (2p). Music was often provided by the Swanage Town Band. The rink later became the Lugano Ballroom. Many will remember Ken Lane and his orchestra. It is now used as a stockroom by Nixons the hardware shop.

7.50 Station Road in the late 1930s. The Grand Cinema is on the far left, and next to it is the Central Garage with the Lugano Ballroom above. The 'Grand' had been converted into a cinema in 1932 with the addition of a projection box on the roof (seen in this photo), part of which survives today. The wooden framework above the frontage seen in the earlier photos had become rotten and was removed.

7.51 Station Road during the flood on 17 November 1935. This gives a closer view of the Central Garage which was replaced by Woolworths in 1952. This closed in December 2008 and during 2009 Nixons Hardware moved here from their previous premises in Mermond Place. The Lugano Ballroom was above the garage and had earlier been the Alhambra Rink (see 7.49).

7.52 Grand Cinema, Station Road, proposed rebuilding plans, 1937. In 1936 the owner of both cinemas local builder Frank Walton sold out to the Portsmouth Town

Cinemas circuit who submitted plans to rebuild the Grand in Art Deco style. These were rejected in 1938 and again in 1949 due to planning difficulties. In April 1953 Tony Whitehouse took over both cinemas and in November closed the Grand. The Swanage Cinema was renamed the Ritz while the Grand became the short-lived Ritz Ballroom and then the dress shop Louise (until the early 1980s). It then became part of the adjoining supermarket.

7.53 Station Road looking east, *c* 1900. On the left is Brook Dairy with Brook Farm behind. These buildings stood on the corner of what is now Mermond Place where Barclays Bank is today. They were demolished in December 1913, followed in January 1914 by the old cottages seen on the right (see 7.57).

7.54 Station Road looking east, 1909. This is a more familiar view and shows the row of shops from Commercial Road along to Institute Road that had just been completed. On the far left is Brook Dairy. The shop on the right is still Brown's, but is now Brown's the opticians rather than Brown's the butchers.

7.55 Charles Brown's butcher's shop, Station Road, *c* 1910. This is a postcard addressed to the Plommer family in Canada who had run the shop from 1893–1906. Charles Brown was a 'Purveyor of Primest English, Scotch and Colonial Meat' with 'Families Waited on Daily for Orders'. His widow Rose carried on the business for many years. The shop is now I.J. Brown, the Weymouth-based opticians.

7.56 Frisby's (Leicester) Boot Stores, Station Road, *c* 1910. This was next door to Charles Brown's butchers shop (above). Frisby's opened this shop in 1893. Their advertising stated they had '90 other Branches' and that 'All Goods are Guaranteed to Wear or Exchanged' with 'everything marked in Plain Figures at Keen Prices'. In 2010 this was still a shoe shop trading as Shoe Zone.

7.57 Station Road looking east towards the Mowlem Institute, *c* 1910. On the left are Harry Smith's fish shop and Brook Cottages, which were demolished in January 1914 and the road widened. Due to outbreak of the First World War and shortage of manpower, new shops were not built on part of this site until the 1920s, shown as waste ground in the next photograph.

7.58 Station Road on Armistice Day, 11 November 1918. The *Swanage Guardian* reported that 'flags were fluttering from every window' and 'after dinner many of the shops closed and the town gave itself up to rejoicing'. In the evening the band of the Tank Corps came down 'followed by a procession of a tank and motor lorries filled with soldiers'.

7.59 The Post Office, Station Road, 1908. This new Post Office was built by Parsons & Hayter and opened in March 1908. It replaced the Office in the lower High Street (see 1.25). The present Post Office in King's Road was opened officially on 14 February 1974. During additions to the building seen here, problems with the foundations led to it being completely dismantled in 2008 and rebuilt. It has been carefully reconstructed using new materials as a virtual replica of the original with a retail shop unit and 12 new apartments named 'Sandcastles'.

7.60 Postmen outside Swanage Post Office, Station Road, 1914. The postmen pose for a photograph before their early morning deliveries. Second from left is Fred Masters. This view can be dated to 1914 by the wooden scaffolding reflected in the windows, where Job Smith's new 'Furnishing Stores' was being built opposite on the corner of Station Road and Shore Road. This was later Fortes (now Funworld Cafe).

7.61 Station Road looking west, *c* 1910. An unusual view showing the present shops on the left with Brook Cottages and Powell's photographic studio on the right. Thomas Powell had set-up his first studio here in 1898. Brook Cottages were demolished in January 1914 and the road widened. Powell's studio was re-erected on Shore Road until he had a permanent shop built. This closed in 1956 (now part of Funworld).

7.62 Station Road after the flood on 9 March 1914. The *Swanage Guardian* reported that at the Post Office (left centre) 'the water almost reached the opening where the letters are dropped in'. On the right, Job Smith's new 'Furnishing Stores' was under construction. The Central Garage (built in 1910) can also be seen beyond this. At the top end of Station Road new shops were being built on the left-hand side.

7.63 Pumping out flood water in Institute Road, 10 March 1914. The fire brigade pumping out one of Jimmy Day's shops (now Ladbrokes). L to R: William Davis White (father of Gideon), Robert Reynolds (owner of the wine shop), Gideon White (fire brigade Captain), Cecil Harding, Victor Harding, George Weeks (man at bank door), Sidney Shelston, Fred Moss, Fred Bennett, Arthur Summers.

7.64 Institute Road on Armistice Day, 11 November 1918. Four years had passed since the above photo was taken and seen a huge loss of life in the 'Great War'. The Swanage War Memorial erected in 1920 records the names of over 90 local men killed during the conflict. Notice the banner 'Pity the Unemployed', a significant problem during the aftermath of the War.

7.65 Carnival procession, *c* 1935. A Carnival Queen, possibly Iris Hopkins, and her Maids of Honour Ruth Pitcher and Peggy Brown are passing the Mowlem Institute. The first Swanage Carnival Queen was Marjorie Smith in 1934. The Southern National bus alongside the Institute is a Leyland 32-seater (registration YC8986).

"DENNIS REDHEAD'S FOOLS IN FANTASY"

7.66 Dennis Redhead's concert party 'Fools in Fantasy' in the late 1930s. They appeared at the Mowlem for three consecutive seasons from 1937 with a 'B.B.C. and West End Cast'. Rex Rashley (back row) had apparently run away from school at 14 and joined a 'variety combination'. In the late 1960s he was on BBC television playing bit parts on *The Morecambe and Wise Show*.

7.67 The Mowlem Institute during demolition, 1965. The Institute was built by John Mowlem for the 'Benefit and Mutual Improvement of the Working Classes, not excluding occasional Meetings on Freemasonry'. It opened on 19 January 1863 and included a reading room and library. The Institute served variously as a theatre, cinema and place for other entertainments, events and meetings for over a century.

7.68 The site of the former Mowlem Institute, 1965. This interesting view also shows the former 'County Bridge' on the left, rebuilt and dated 1910. The present theatre was constructed by local builders Jefferson Pond. It was officially opened on 11 May 1967. Films were shown from 1969, with a projection box added to the roof.

7.69 Institute Road looking across the old 'County Bridge', 1905. This carried a notice threatening transportation for malicious damage! The right-hand wall was removed when James Day's second shop was built in 1906, although the lower courses still remain under the present pavement. His other shop the Durlston Dairy and Isle of Purbeck Fruit Stores (on the far right) was designed by Clifton and Robinson in 1898.

7.70 Institute Road, 1911. The shops on the left were built by Parsons & Hayter (nos 1–7 in 1899 and 9–25 in 1904/05). Note the selection of postcards in the window of Misses L & E White's shop on the corner. This building was taken over by The Capital & Counties Bank in 1915 and became the Westminster Bank in 1921. It was destroyed in the air raid on 17 August 1942 when the bank manager Horace Mills was killed.

7.71 Hill & Churchill, Institute Road, *c* **1905.** Eliza Hill and Emma Churchill started their booksellers and stationers in Station Road during 1893 and moved here in 1899. The shop included a 'Library in connection with Mudie and Tabard Inn' and an 'Art Needlework Depot'. In the mid 1930s the business moved to James Day's former shop at 6 Institute Road, recently vacated by the Domestic Bazaar Co. Ltd. The name Hill & Churchill's is still familiar to many local residents, although the shop was taken over by Martin's the newsagents from 1980/81.

7.72 George Beer's Oriental Café, Vienna House, Institute Road, *c* **1910**. George Beer was a pastry cook and confectioner who started his business in 1886 and moved to this shop from the High Street in 1902. He won many awards for his bread including a 'Gold Medal and Diploma' in 1901. This café was run on strictly 'oriental lines'.

7.73 Silver Jubilee of King George V, Institute Road, 6 May 1935. The *Dorset County Chronicle* reported that 'Swanage looked so gay and impressive in carnival dress'. The Council Chairman James Smith and Town Clerk Thomas Arnold visited Herston School and presented the children with souvenir propelling pencils. Note the 'Stop Me and Buy One' ice cream vendor, a familiar sight in the 1930s.

7.74 Institute Road in the 1930s. The Westminster Bank on the right received a direct hit during the air raid on 17 August 1942. In the centre is Southern National bus AEC Regal (registration TK 4883) outside the Mowlem Institute, departure point for the service to Weymouth. On the corner of Shore Road was Job Smith's 'Furnishing Stores' which had a roof 'Tea Garden'.

7.75 Institute Road after the air raid on 17 August 1942. A single high-explosive bomb was dropped at 12.35 pm, a few minutes before the air raid siren sounded. The Westminster Bank on the corner together with Bruton's the ironmongers and Espley's the chemists were destroyed. A second bomb was dropped on Chapel Lane (see also 2.10).

7.76 Institute Road after the air raid, 1942. This view from Muspratt's photographic studio shows the remains of the Westminster Bank, Bruton's and Espley's. The fatal casualties were the bank manager Horace Mills and three Air Raid Wardens (Alec Bruton, his sister Nora and Kathleen Winsome Hawkins).

7.77 Silver Jubilee of King George V, Institute Road, May 1935. The *Dorset County Chronicle* reported that 'principal streets and particularly Institute Road were brilliantly

decorated with its scores of flags and garlands of red, white and blue festoons'. At 10 pm scouts lit the Jubilee Beacon on North Hill. The headmaster of Herston School, Mr Butler, said 'the King's reign had been a very harassing time in peace and war, but they were looking forward to a permanent peace, so that when the children grew up they would not have the strife faced by some of their elders'.

7.78 Muspratt's photographic studio, May 1937. Helen Muspratt had moved her studio here from lower High Street. Her sister Joan ran the business in Swanage from the 1930s until she died in 1958. The studio eventually closed in December 1962. The next two photos show the remains of the shop front after the air raid of 17 August 1942.

7.79 Institute Road after the air raid on 17 August 1942. This view shows the blast damage from the bomb which fell on the Westminster Bank opposite. From right to left these buildings were: stationers Hill & Churchill, Hayman's Café and Muspratt's studio, all of which were later repaired and Hayman's Café is still in business today.

7.80 Institute Road 5 days after the air raid, 1942. Compared with the above view some repair work had already been carried out, with scaffolding around Hill & Churchill's shop front and some of their upstairs windows reglazed. The overall casualty figures in this air raid were 8 killed and 39 wounded.

7.81 Coronation decorations in Institute Road, May 1937. Two years after the Silver Jubilee the streets were once again decorated. King George V died in January 1936

and in December King Edward VIII abdicated in order to marry American divorcee Wallis Simpson. At the time of the Coronation of King George VI in May 1937, Baptist Minister Rev. Stanley Smith said 'in spite of the upheavals among the nations of the world, the Throne of England remained so stable'. Notice that horse-drawn vehicles had not yet given over entirely to the motor car.

7.82 Decorations in The Square, May 1937. Randalls the chemists is on the left (now Surprise 'N' Store). In the centre is the Trocadero Restaurant (now New Look) and on the right the White Swan Inn. Events on Coronation Day 12 May included a 'Procession and Carnival' around the town at 6.30 pm which was 'practically spoilt' by 'drenching rain from start to finish'.

7.83 The severe storm on 24 August 1931. The *Swanage Times* stated that the storm 'exceeded anything that can be remembered'. The Nineham family's sailing and motor boat *Arab* (seen here) was hauled up the slipway minus her rudder and only slightly damaged. However, local fishermen Charlie Brown and Bill Brown lost their sailing boats *Neptune* and *Mary Ann*, 'broken to pieces by the fury of the waves'.

7.84 The Parade during the flood on 17 November 1935. It was described in the *Swanage Times* as 'a miniature Niagara'. After the overnight flood on 2 September 1939 Ron Hardy was in his boat the next morning and saw new shirts washed into the sea from one of the gentlemen's outfitters. Then he heard that Prime Minister Neville Chamberlain had announced that from 11 am Britain was at war with Germany.

Swanage Museum Local Studies Centre

This offers a wide range of resources for local and family history research. These resources have been used extensively during preparation of this book, and include photographs, local newspapers on microfilm, large-scale Ordnance Survey maps, street directories, rate books, trade directories index, pub landlords index and building plans index.

Access to the Local Studies Centre, Marine Villas on Swanage Pier is by appointment only (tel. 01929 423850, email: swanagemuseum@swanagemuseum.plus.com). Research enquiries can also be made at the Swanage Museum & Heritage Centre, The Square via the Museum website (www.swanagemuseum.co.uk).

Selected Bibliography and Other Sources of Information

Bean, O.R., *A B C Guide to Swanage*, 1906–1936.

Benfield, E., *Purbeck Shop*, Cambridge University Press 1940, 1948, (reprint 1990).

Borrett, S., *Swanage in the 1920's and 1930's*, Amberwood Graphics 2002.

Borrett, S., *Swanage in World War II*, Amberwood Graphics 2010.

Dalton, D., *The First Hundred Years, The Baptist Cause in Swanage from 1905*, 2004.

Hardy, W. Masters, *Smuggling Days in Purbeck*, Dorset County Chronicle 1906, 1907 (reprint 1978).

Hardy, W. Masters, *Old Swanage & Purbeck*, Dorset County Chronicle 1908, 1910 (reprint 1979).

Haysom, D. & Bragg, D., *Swanage and Purbeck in Old Photographs*, Alan Sutton 1991.

Haysom, D. & Parker, J., *Last Days of Steam in Dorset & Bournemouth*, Alan Sutton 1993.

Haysom, D. & Patrick, J., *Swanage in Old Picture Postcards*, European Library 1993.

Jackson, B., *Swanage 125 Years of Railways*, Oakwood Press 2010.

Legg, R., *Purbeck Island*, Dorset Publishing Company 1972, 1989.

Legg, R., *The Book of Swanage*, Halsgrove Publishing 2001.

Lewer, D., *John Mowlem's Swanage*, Dorset Publishing Company 1990.

Lewer, D. & Calkin, J.B, *Curiosities of Swanage*, Friary Press/Purbeck Press 1971–2007.

Lewer, D. & Smale, D., *Swanage Past*, Phillimore 1994, 2004.

Mitchell, V. & Smith, K., *Branch Line to Swanage*, Middleton Press 1986, 1989.

Musk, J., *Lesser Known Swanage*, Roving Press 2009.

Woods, R., *A History of Swanage United Reformed Church*, 2005.

Daily Echo, Bournemouth (Scott Harrison, Chief Librarian); *Dorset County Chronicle* (1823–1957); Dorset History Centre; *Swanage & Wareham Guardian* (1889–1928); *Swanage Times* (1919–83); Swanage Town Hall archives (Dr Martin Ayres, Acting Town Clerk); *Wareham and Isle of Purbeck Advertiser* (J.W. Tribbett, 1879–89).

Other Roving Press Titles

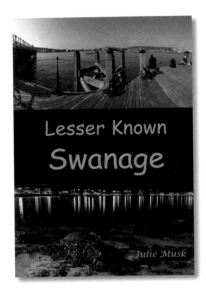

'*I think it is the most interesting book about the town that I have read.*'
(Lin Dorey, Swanage resident)

'*Although I have been to Swanage many times it's amazing...how unobservant I have been when walking around. The walks are all short and easily manageable and... it gained me access to the Purbeck Hotel to look around...you will get so much more from your visit!*'
(Amazon Review)

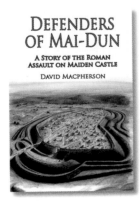